D1740131

Higher Education Governance
in the Arab World

To my dedicated colleagues, partners, and everyone who contributed to the achievement of this book . . . Thank you

Contents

List of Figures

List of Tables

The Impact of Governance in Higher Education Institutions
on Scientific Research in the Arab World

The Role of Governance in Promoting the Presence of Women
in Higher Education Institutions in the Arab World

Introduction

Georges Azzi

A Theoretical Overview

If the twentieth century is considered the age of management discipline, the late twentieth century and the early twenty-first century are seen to be the era of governance; the latter is a central preoccupation for researchers, corporate and public governors, and activists. Governance is used to designate the "art or manner of governing" by engaging a participating civil society at national and international levels. Thus, governance is the rule of the rule and the management of the management relevant to the large scope of institutions. The etymological origins of the word governance can be traced to the Greek verb "Kybernein," which means "to steer a vessel or a float" (Campbell and Carayannis 2012). If, in the marine world, navigating a ship is the challenge and responsibility of the captain, enabling the ship to arrive safely and at the right destination, in the business world, governors are obliged to help corporations achieve their objectives.

G. Azzi (✉)
Holy Spirit University of Kaslik (USEK), Jounieh, Lebanon
e-mail: georgesazzi@usek.edu.lb

© The Author(s) 2018
G. Azzi (ed.), *Higher Education Governance in the Arab World*,
DOI 10.1007/978-3-319-52060-5_1

Corporate governance determines the direction and performance of a corporation through both structure and relationships. On the one hand, it entails direction, administration, and control techniques. It is concerned with the elaboration and implementation of the corporation's goals and objectives. On the other hand, corporate governance also involves relationships among different stakeholders, whether internal or external parties. The board of directors (BoD) or the board of trustees (BoT) is the central body of governance activities. The implementation of board governance rules and regulations is ensured by its critical relationships, primarily those with shareholders and the management body. In other words, it is the combination of tools that protects stakeholders. Applying agency theory, governance means guaranteeing that the management entity (or agent) runs and manages the organization for the maximum benefit of one or numerous stakeholders (or principals) within a legal, supervisory, official, and ethical framework. Included among the many stakeholders are shareholders, financial institutions and banks, suppliers, clients, employees, and any other party that is affected by the decisions of corporations.

Governance decisions determine the success or failure of a company. In consequence, as per many researchers, defiance in governance bodies and systems leads to failure of corporations (Beer 2003).

Governance practices ensure accountability and transparency, which are necessary in today's businesses.

In the conditions in which all industries are currently operating, all businesses have to adapt to globalization and its rapid rhythm of change and development. Far more than ever, corporate governance is proving to be the preeminent instrument for keeping up with all these old-new rules.

A Theoretical Overview: Principles

The 2015 report by the Organisation for Economic Co-operation and Development (OECD) addressed to the G20 finance ministers and central bank governors presents six principles for corporate governance. It outlines an effective and efficient corporate governance structure;

it defines the rightful treatment of all shareholders and major ownership functions and the relationship with institutional investors, stock markets, and any other intermediaries; and it also explains the function of stakeholders and the requirement for transparency, responsibility, and accountability by the board (OECD 2015).

To begin with, ensuring a good base for corporate governance structure is a necessity: this promotes effectiveness and efficiency. In the market, it maintains transparency, fairness, and consistency in the distribution of the available resources. The framework for corporate governance should conform with local and international law through precise implementation and supervision. Since corporate governance practices have significant influence, their impact on the market—especially on global economic and financial performance and the promotion of integrity through participants' motivations, transparency, and market activity—should be taken into account. In a successful corporation's implementation of governance principles and rules, responsibilities are clearly stated and divided among different authorities in the best interests of the public. Power, reliability, and resources are a must in order for administrators, managers, monitors, and any other executive authority to perform and meet their obligations professionally. No ambiguity concerning decisions is acceptable; all resolutions should be suitable to a precise time, well and fully explained, transparent, and certainly not in service to hidden agendas. A corporate governance model achieves good results based on the gathering and analysis of a large volume of information. For this reason information must flow and be accessible to the relevant decision-makers. The potential problem of asymmetric information should be continually addressed in order to ensure an unrestricted exchange of information.

Furthermore, one of the primary responsibilities of corporate governance is to protect the interests of shareholders. It also aims to protect their rights and interests. The basic rights of shareholders include protection of ownership records, transmission of their shares, procurement of information on a regular basis, participation in general shareholders' meetings and elections, election and elimination of board members, and receipt of their portion of the corporation's profits. All shareholders from the same class should be treated equally. They should benefit from the same rights and advantages. Concerning minorities, corporate governance practices protect and defend in particular minority shareholders, since they are potentially subject, directly or indirectly, to abusive actions by a larger group of shareholders. Majorities are tempted to impose rules that maximize their own benefits; in order to compensate minorities and maintain a balance, abusive practices should be prohibited.

Moreover, organizational investors, stock markets, and intermediaries are as concerned as any other party with the corporate governance of a firm. Rigorous economic and financial incentives are needed. The interests of consultants, experts, brokers, traders, and rating agencies should converge with those of investors. On the basis of honesty and reliability, corporate governance has the role and responsibility of providing accurate listings and reasonable and real stock prices on local and international stock markets.

Additionally, corporate governance highlights the role of stakeholders. The rights of stakeholders are established and protected either by law or through reciprocal agreements. Collaboration between the company and the stakeholders is beneficial for all parties. By applying the stakeholder theory to corporate governance, all stakeholders participate in the process of corporate governance; access to relevant information, regularly and in a timely manner, must be provided. Stakeholders—such as employees, non-governmental organizations (NGOs), creditors, banks and financial institutions, suppliers, and any other party that might be influenced by the firm's decisions—should be able to share their concerns about illegal or unethical practices with the board or any relevant public authorities, without any restrictions or risk of losing their rights.

In addition, in order to feel secure, the public needs access to internal information. Therefore, such information should be frequently distributed. The corporation should be committed to making accurate and relevant disclosures concerning its financial situation, performance, ownership, and management. It should also include objectives and non-financial information, remuneration of key persons on the board or at the executive level, new or omitted rules and regulations, and all governance structures and procedures. Those reports containing financial or non-financial information should be inspected by internal and external auditors. In an efficient form of governance, external auditors are independent and competent to present the reality objectively; they are also accountable to the shareholders. Those reports and disclosures should be available at any time to all stakeholders.

Last but not least, the board, being the center of governance, has significant responsibilities. It creates the strategic framework for the company and monitors the management body. It is accountable to both the company and the company's shareholders; it works in an honest and devoted way and cares for the interests of the company and shareholders alike. Its work is critical, and therefore board members should maintain high ethical standards. Their work covers different key functions; some of these have already been mentioned, since the board is involved in all the previous principles. For example, it is their duty to create, review, and align financial and non-financial procedures: strategies, plans, risk management, objectives, budgets, and policies. Furthermore, their work is not restricted to theoretical issues; they are also involved in monitoring, implementing, and adjusting the firm's governance. The board and its members should have the ability to see and judge the corporation objectively and independently; for this reason it should be divided into various specialized committees, and many of its members should be non-executives and outsiders. To ensure effective governance, the board conducts regular evaluations to assess their performance and to check whether they have the right combination of competences to perform their tasks.

A Worldwide Overview: Reform of Corporations

Worldwide reforms are not born out of a void. Reforms are initiated after significant corporate scandals, which can happen anywhere and at any time. Regardless of whether the scandal results from intentional or accidental action taken by the corporation and its people, it can be noticed that large-scale scandals that affect either the local or the international market are primarily related to governance rules and practices. On the one hand, consequences may cover corporate governance rules and practices; for example, if the CEO and/or the governance board is changed, the key persons are replaced, and so on. On the other hand, the consequences of a scandal can take place on governmental and national levels, such as strict application of the existing law, enhancement of new rules and penalties, and enforcement of strong government control through its different divisions.

A Worldwide Overview: Reform in Higher Education Institutions

Governance is subject to reforms across the world but follows different rhythms in each country and in different sectors. Governance is subject to reforms in many other sectors beyond corporations. We are interested here in reviewing governance reforms in higher education institutions.

Higher education is facing an increasing number of challenges. Within its international framework, governance in higher education entities is mainly concerned with two issues: how to preserve an academic environment that is favorable for scholars and scientists, and how to face the challenges of the twenty-first century, from mass higher education to financial, business, and social realities (Al-Rashdan 2009). Well-known higher education experts are aware of the importance of implementing governance to achieve both ends. Worldwide, governance rules are being developed and practices are being implemented, including in the higher education system.

Situational Overview: Arab Higher Education Governance

If governance in international higher education institutions is of particular importance, what is the situation in the Arab world?

The region is characterized by the peculiarities among the Arab world—differences in political systems, cultures, interests, and concerns—which have created numerous conflicts. Indeed, it is clear that the Arab world is facing a deficiency in governance in many sectors, including higher education. Higher education is the fountain from which society draws its future leaders and addresses the needs of the society (Altman 1996). Thus, Arab society needs more than ever to strengthen its higher education governance in order to meet today's challenges and demands.

We believe that higher education institutions are agents of change and provide fertile ground for innovation and development. Based on the discussion so far, what are the challenges that higher education institutions must overcome in order to achieve governance reform?

This book is an attempt to elaborate on the current situation of governance in higher education institutions in the Arab world and to stimulate reforms. The authors hope to steer the Arab world toward more governance in higher education institutions, and even to leading and affecting the whole higher education governance system.

Book Contribution

Many sectors in the Arab world, including that of higher education, currently lack governance and are in urgent need of reform. The market needs a reference work with a broader perspective that provides insights from the real world, written by international professionals and generating hope for a better future by presenting a clear road map. With the increasing requirements for accreditation and international partnerships, Arab higher education institutions need to strengthen their internal governance to meet those new challenges and offer hope for a brighter future. This book will also contribute further information in the research field, since it covers a large, diverse, and rich body of knowledge and information about the subject.

This book is unique in the authenticity and timeliness of the subject, its diverse array of themes and approaches, and its enriching perspectives. It gathers experts from the fields of education and governance—including professionals, academics, and NGO initiators—and puts a special focus on the Arab region. Thanks to its unique perspective, the book will expand the scope of discussion and reveal potential new areas of interest for researchers.

It will reduce ambiguity about the topic of governance, and consequently foster real change toward better governance in the region, especially in higher education institutions.

Readers and Beneficiaries

This book will be of interest to all experts in the field of education and/or business management and especially in governance. It will help higher education directors, managers, and potential employees to understand and improve their institutions. It is also addressed to activists and members of NGOs, from both Arab and other nationalities, who are working toward a better education system nationally within the Arab world and/or internationally. The book will be an important reference work for public bodies, such as the education ministries in the Arab world. Indeed, it will be of interest to higher education institutions, research centers, and laboratories for research purposes. Any organization, operating locally and/or internationally, that is involved in accreditations, rankings, and quality education will benefit from reading this book. In general, all stakeholders in higher education institutions are potential readers and beneficiaries of this book.

The topics discussed are as follows:

Internationalization and Globalization, and their Effect on Higher Education Institutions in the Arab World—*Imad-eddine Hatimi*

"Zero-Based" Governance: A New Model for the Future—*Nabil A. Husni*

The Impact of Governance in Higher Education Institutions on Scientific Research in the Arab World—*Elie Bouri and Mirine Maalouf*

Governance Reform in Higher Education Institutions in the Arab World: An Institutional Initiative—*Shafig Al-Haddad and Ayman Yasin*

The Role of Governments in Shaping Governance of Higher Education Institutions in the Arab World—*Antoine Habchi*

Educational Reform, Privatization, and the Challenge of Collaborative Governance in Higher Education in the Arab World—*John Willoughby*

The Role of Governance in Promoting the Presence of Women in Higher Education Institutions in the Arab World—*Madonna Salameh and Diala Kozaily*

The Role of Religious Organizations Running Higher Education Institutions in the Arab World in Governance Reform—*Georges Azzi*

References

Al-Rashdan, A. A. (2009). Higher education in the Arab world: Hopes and challenges. *Arab Insight*, *2*(6), 77–90.

Altman, I. (1996). Higher education and psychology in the millennium. *American Psychologist*, *51*(4), 371.

Beer, M. (2003). Why total quality management programs do not persist: The role of management quality and implications for leading a TQM transformation. *Decision Sciences*, *34*(4), 623–642.

Campbell, D. F., and Carayannis, E. G. (2012). Conceptual definition of two key terms: Governance and higher education. In *Epistemic governance in higher education* (pp. 3–11). New York: Springer.

OECD (2015). G20/OECD Principles of corporate governance. Paper presented at the G20 finance ministers and central bank governance meeting, Ankara, September 4–5.

Georges Azzi is an Associate Professor of Finance at the Holy Spirit University of Kaslik (USEK). Former Dean of the Faculty of Business and Commercial Sciences, he is currently Head of the Doctoral Commission at the Faculty of Business and Commercial Sciences, and the Vice President for Finance at USEK. He is also a member of the Editorial Committee of the *Arab Economic and Business Journal* (AEBJ), and has published several peer-reviewed articles.

Internationalization and Globalization, and their Effect on Higher Education Institutions in the Arab World

Imad-eddine Hatimi

Our world has undergone significant change as a result of internationalization and globalization. According to Daly (1999), the former phenomenon usually refers to the increasingly strong interrelationships between countries, whereas the latter represents the integration of their activities into a single global market. Internationalization relies on the multiplication of exchanges, whereas globalization is achieved once there is free circulation of people and capital together with more easily conducted business transactions.

Technically speaking, both phenomena are measured by means of economic and social indicators. In this context, five economic indicators are to be singled out, linked to international trade (import/export), foreign direct investments, the level of employment generated by international companies, foreign participation in research and development (R&D) activities, and the added value brought by international

I.-e. Hatimi (✉)
ESCA Ecole de Management, Casablanca, Morocco
e-mail: ihatimi@esca.ma

© The Author(s) 2018

G. Azzi (ed.), *Higher Education Governance in the Arab World*,
DOI 10.1007/978-3-319-52060-5_2

companies (International Monetary Fund (IMF) 2008). From a social point of view, indicators might be those linked to population movements and the circulation of information throughout the world.

In this chapter, we will first review the economicnd social impact of internationalization and globalization on the world as a whole, and on the Arab world in particular. Next, we will give an account of how the internationalization of the higher education (HE) sector has occurred around the world. Finally, we will propose a strategy that the Arab world and their HE institutions could adopt to meet the challenges posed by globalization and internationalization, based on their present positioning as regards both phenomena.

Internationalization and Globalization: Economic and Cultural Impacts

Whatever distinction is made between internationalization and globalization, it is clear that both phenomena remain interdependent and critical to explaining the major economic and social transformations that have occurred at the global level in a matter of a few decades.

At the economic level, the process of internationalization has been brought about by the multiplication of alliances and trade exchanges. As an illustration, the percentage of exports in world gross domestic product (GDP) has risen from 19.6% in 1990 to 29.3% in 2015 (World Bank 2016). This trend has escalated thanks to the signing of several bilateral free trade agreements and the creation of areas with free circulation of goods and people (North American Free Trade Agreement (NAFTA), European Union (EU), etc.), the harmonization of laws and standards at the international level, and the unification of financial markets. The removal of quotas and customs tariffs on imports and the creation of free trade zones have enabled multinationals to manufacture and sell in different countries, and even to benefit from advantages in some instances.

As a consequence, national borders in the various markets have disappeared, allowing for the emergence of a globalized market in which the various economies operate as both consumers and producers.

One need only recall that international trade accounts for about two-thirds of global GDP and that both emerging and developing countries produce over 80% of the world's growth (IMF 2016). As for foreign direct investments, they have continually increased through the creation of new companies abroad and, more recently, through the acquisition of companies in other countries (Organisation for Economic Co-operation and Development (OECD) 2010). Nowadays, they concern not only the setting up of delocalized production units, but also R&D activities. In fact, at least 15% of R&D spending in countries such as Austria, the UK, Slovakia, Hungary, Canada, and the Netherlands (OECD 2010) is from abroad.

The Arab world have not remained unaffected by the two phenomena. They have multiplied their cooperation links, alliances, and trade exchanges with one another and the rest of the world. International trade (import/export) accounts for 93.6% of GDP in the Arab world, which is higher than the world average (57.9%), whereas it was running at 70% only 15 years ago (World Bank 2016). The percentage of exports in GDP has doubled since 1986 and reached 50.9% in 2014 in the Arab world (World Bank 2016). Imports amounted to 42.7% of the Arab world's GDP, compared to 29.6% in the world in general.

Thus, the Arab world have felt the impact of globalization as a result of their economic integration with other areas of the world (the Gulf states, the EU, North America, etc.) through free trade agreements (Morocco recording over 56 such agreements), free trade areas (e.g., the United Arab Emirates (UAE)), and unified markets (Gulf states). The International Logistics Performance Index for the Arab world is 2.9, above that at the global level, which shows the connectivity of this region to the world economy (World Bank 2016).

Consequently, the Arab world have had to position themselves within a global market. In fact, from an economic point of view, internationalization and globalization have undoubtedly enabled the Arab world to access a larger market where they can sell their natural resources, which are quite plentiful, and offer their cheaper production lines and human resources.

Unfortunately, the Arab world do not capture a significant enough share of this global market. For instance, fewer than three

Arab-world companies were listed in the Global Fortune 500 in 2015. Moreover, over the years, internationalization and globalization processes have given rise to free trading and international competition. They have brought about new key factors for economic growth, namely investment and production factors with value added. In fact, with the drop in oil prices, the Arab world have had to set up a competitive economy based on a business context that is favorable to foreign investment, with skilled human resources and innovative products and services that are able to meet the demands of international customers.

In this sense, the Arab world need a high-quality HE system that can meet the quantitative and qualitative challenges of internationalization and globalization. HE institutions in the Arab world should help business organizations develop international links and adopt practices and techniques that are recognized at the international level.

From a social point of view, internationalization and globalization have also affected the various countries, since they have encouraged their populations to open up to the world, thanks to the introduction of new technologies and the mobility of people between countries.

Access to social media networks, and to the Web in the wider sense, has allowed people to share their cultures and to take part in the emergence of a universal identity. Such a trend, which was triggered by satellite television and the telephone, has increased with Internet access and, above all, with the arrival of social networks. The number of Internet users in the world has risen rapidly since 2000,[1] increasing from 6.8% to 40.7% of the population in 15 years. In the Arab world, it reached 34.5% in 2015 against only 1.1% in 2000 (World Bank 2016). In 2014, there were on average 109 telephone subscribers per 100 people (World Bank 2016). In Morocco, there are more telephone subscribers than potential voters. In 2016, there were around 44 Internet users per 100 people in the Middle East and North Africa (MENA) region, according to the World Bank (2016).

---

[1] Internet users are individuals who have used the Internet (from any location) in the last 12 months.

Moreover, people's mobility between countries has contributed to the mix of cultures, thus achieving the progressive globalization of values in Arab-world societies, though not without producing internal frictions. On the one hand, the number of tourists visiting the Arab world has risen from 34 million to 83 million in only 15 years (World Bank 2016). On the other hand, the percentage of the population born to foreign nationals in the Arab world rose from 5.8% in 2000 to 8.9% in 2015, a ratio that is higher than the world average of 3.3% (World Bank 2016).

Furthermore, access to the various cultures in the world through modern means of communication has led Arab youth to adopt the universal values of freedom and equality. However, cultural globalization is not universally supported in the Arab world; it also faces popular resistance in response to fears about the future of national identities.

Given the aforementioned economic and social trends generated by the effects of internationalization and globalization, it is evident that the world and the Arab world have experienced a major evolution. In the next section, we will describe how this has affected the HE sector.

Internationalization of HE

Following the pattern that has occurred at the economic and social levels, the HE sector has also experienced the effects of internationalization and globalization. In fact, the internationalization of HE has come as a response to both phenomena.

As regards the HE sector, the word "internationalization" means "the process of integrating an international, intercultural, or global dimension into the purpose, functions or delivery of post-secondary education" (Knight 2008, p. 21). This process has, on the one hand, encouraged HE institutions to reinforce their activities outside the domestic market, in terms of international mobility of students and faculty, or training and/or research programs. On the other hand, it has encouraged them to incorporate locally the international issues raised in their immediate environment in their course topics and in faculty research and publications.

In a study carried out by the International Association of Universities (IAU), out of 6,800 institutions surveyed, 53% had an internationalization strategy and 23% were currently elaborating one (IAU 2014). Furthermore, based on the same study, 61% of the institutions surveyed had budgets earmarked for internationalization. This demonstrates the engagement of universities and schools across the world as regards internationalization. In the case of business schools, Iniguez (2012) identified four main ways of achieving global presence, depending on level of risk: 1) multi-campus Strategy, 2) mergers and acquisitions, 3) online and blended programs, and 4) international alliances.

As a matter of fact, since the role of academic institutions is to respond to socioeconomic conditions in their countries, they have taken into account the stakes of internationalization and globalization in their teaching and research activities. Thus, HE institutions have sought to support the development of their countries by helping them understand how to benefit from the opening up of new markets and global economic integration, and also to manage the risks involved in interdependence whenever major crises arise.

According to the IAU survey, the external factors driving this internationalization process are mostly linked to governmental policies and the needs of the industrial world (IAU 2014). The demands of international accreditation organizations represent a third source of pressure to justify the internationalization of HE.

For instance, HE institutions in management education have tried to develop and teach the knowledge required for doing business abroad and even in specific contexts, such as Latin American and Asia, given their huge market potential. They have also tackled critical topics such as those related to the fact that countries have become interdependent. One need only recall the impact of the financial crisis, which was triggered in the USA, on other regions in the world. HE management institutions have also complied with the promotion of the international dimension by some international accreditation bodies, such as the European Foundation for Management Development (EFMD).

As regards the benefits targeted by academic institutions through the internationalization process, the IAU survey showed that the development of a global perspective among students appears to be the primary aim, followed by the determination to improve the quality of their teaching, whereas the search for additional income came up last. For members of the Association to Advance Collegiate Schools of Business (AACSB),[2] four motivations are behind the globalization of management education, namely the global nature of business, the global market for talent, the need for intercultural awareness, and the opportunity for global exchanges with other institutions in the HE sector (AACSB 2011).

Thus, the development of a global perspective among students seems to be very important for the business world, if we consider how the internationalization of HE has contributed to graduate employability. A survey by the SOCRATES ERASMUS program showed that international mobility is regarded positively by employers (CHE Consult et al. 2014). Graduates who have taken a study stay or an internship abroad have 50% less risk of experiencing long-term unemployment than those with a solely domestic study path. Furthermore, the unemployment rate among the former group after five years is lower by 23%.

On that basis, HE internationalization strategies have been mobilized to this end. First of all, grant and recruitment schemes (Campus France, NCUK, etc.) have been set up to encourage regional and international student enrollment. Second, inter-country agreements and/or governmental strategies have encouraged the opening of international campuses in various countries. Third, several funding programs have enabled scientific research programs to be carried out. Finally, cooperation agreements have been signed to foster faculty and academic staff exchanges (ERASMUS, ERASMUS+, etc.) and the extension of their competencies (trainer training programs), together with administrative skills (transfer of best management practices, etc.).

---

[2] The Association to Advance Collegiate Schools of Business (AACSB) is the world's largest business accreditation network, with more than 1,500 member institutions and organizations in over 90 countries.

In parallel, alignment processes for educational systems at the international level have played a major role in creating a homogeneous educational system that would facilitate the validation of learning outcomes in the various institutions. The main example to be quoted in this respect is the Bologna Process and its "Bachelor, Master, Doctorate" (BMD) scheme, which was first adopted at the European level and then in other regions of the world (Africa, Latin America, and Asia). In this way, national and international accreditation organizations have indeed played a major role in the development of a global HE industry.

Nowadays, the HE market has become integrated at the global level. The training available to students goes beyond the borders of their home countries. Universities and schools are already required to position themselves in a market that comprises both domestic and international competition. One only need consider the significant increase in student mobility over the last few decades. Between 2000 and 2011, the number of students on an international mobility scheme had doubled (UNESCO 2014). In 2013, the number of international students rose to 4.1 million, that is, about 2% of the total number of students in the world (UNESCO Institute for Lifelong Learning (UIL) 2014). This figure should reach seven million by 2020, according to Altbach et al. (2009). In this sense, social sciences, management (business), and law are the most popular areas of study internationally (representing 30% of all international students) (UNESCO Institute for Lifelong Learning (UIL) 2014).

The USA and Europe hold a major share of this market. In 2013, about half of international students were studying in countries like the USA (19%), the UK (10%), France (6%), Australia (6%), Germany (5%), and Italy (2%). Those countries developed intensive strategies focused on internationalization many years ago. One should also note that English-speaking destinations (the USA, the UK, Australia, etc.) hold a dominant position in this market, in spite of the emergence of Latin America and Asia Pacific. As regards France, incoming international mobility has traditionally originated mostly from countries with which France has historical and cultural links, above all from former colonies. In these countries, the French secondary education system is represented by local branches (Algeria, Morocco, Tunisia, Senegal, Ivory

Coast, etc.). In addition, it is facilitated by low tuition fees for foreign students. Some countries, such as Germany, have adopted a long-term strategy focused on the setting up of a network of "ambassadors" in their home countries.

Thus, such a market has become lucrative enough to attract new players, such as Canada, Japan, Russia, and Spain, on top of the traditional destinations (the USA, the UK, France, and Australia). On the whole, the initial intention of countries and their institutions is certainly to attract the best foreign candidates, to promote their values and their practices, and/or to establish influence networks in students' countries of origin by training the elite. However, nowadays, this intention has been turned into a foreign student recruitment strategy in order to generate additional revenues. This is all the more important when one takes into account that several countries apply higher tuition fees for foreign students, which allows them to maintain lower tuition fees for national students.

For instance, in 2014/2015, the 974,926 foreign students who were studying at American universities generated some USD 30 billion, according to the Institute of International Education (2015). In Canada, the revenues generated by foreign students through tuition fees, accommodation, and living expenses totaled about USD 6.2 billion in 2010 (Global Affairs Canada 2012). This activity created 81,000 jobs and generated USD 341 million for state finances.

However, international mobility must overcome some obstacles, such as the lack of financial resources to extend the global experience to more students, local regulations as regards the quality of HE in some countries, and international competition that has become increasingly keen (IAU 2014).

Broadly speaking, this part of our chapter has shown how the HE sector has been affected by internationalization and globalization. It has indicated the extent to which it is very important for HE institutions to incorporate the international dimension in their missions. The promotion of international mobility among students and faculty and the internationalization of the training on offer are excellent ways for HE institutions to develop a global perspective among their graduates, to improve the quality of teaching, and to generate supplementary revenues. In the next part, we will show how HE institutions in the Arab world are seizing opportunities for internationalization and globalization to enhance the growth of their respective countries.

Internationalization of the HE Sector in the Arab World

As Romani (2012) pointed out, the internationalization of HE is in no way a new phenomenon. One need only recall the foundation in 1865 of the Syrian Protestant College, which was to become the American University in Beirut, or the foundation of the Université Saint Joseph, ten years later, by the French Jesuit Mission. However, this trend has had to cope with nationalist currents in the Arab world. In fact, after the Second World War and their attainment of independence, Arab governments were banking on the educational sector to forge a national identity by adopting a policy of opening up HE to all. As a result, the number of Arab universities rose from ten in 1940 to 140 in 2000 and 270 in 2007 (Romani 2012).

In terms of the phenomena of internationalization and globalization, the HE sector in the Arab world is not very significant (Fig. 1). On the one hand, in spite of extensive globalization in the Arab world, their academic institutions have not succeeded in attracting a considerable number of international students. In 2013, the Arab world attracted around 280,300 students from international flows, compared with around 1.83 million in Europe and Central Asia, 919,772 in North America, and 782,775 in East Asia and the Pacific. In addition, in terms of growth, the inbound mobility rate in the Arab world has been around 3%, compared with 4.31% in North America and 4.75% in Europe and Central Asia. In addition, it is important to note that in 2010,[3] only four countries (Egypt, Lebanon, Jordan, and Saudi Arabia) accounted for 83% of inbound international mobility in tertiary education in the region (World Bank 2016).

---

[3] The most recent data available for the different countries.

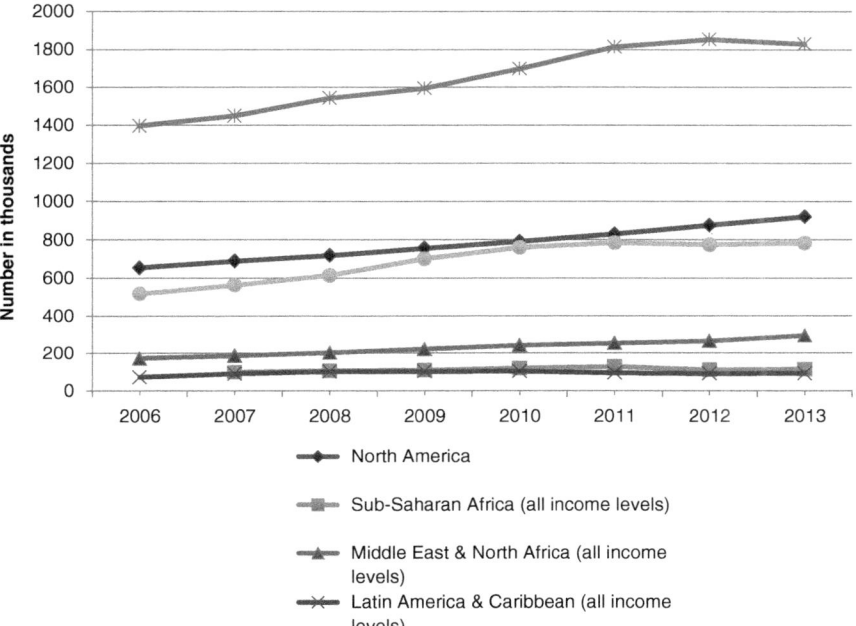

Fig. 1 Total inbound internationally mobile students, from both sexes (in thousands)

Note: This graph was generated by Kneoma (http://knoema.fr/WBEDS2016Apr/education-statistics-world-bank-june-2016), based on World Bank Data (June 2016)

In this way, it appears that the political instability and security issues in some of these countries, especially after the Arab Spring in Egypt and Tunisia, have negatively impacted the attractiveness of the region. Alongside this, the Arab region has experienced, during the last five years, continuing civil wars in Syria and Yemen, and the terrorism threat posed by Al-Qaeda and ISIL in the Arabian Peninsula. The average of the Global Peace Index for the MENA region was around 2.554 in 2015, compared with 1.771 for North America and 1.66 for Europe. Consequently, inbound mobility in Egypt, Lebanon, and Tunisia has decreased since 2011 (Fig. 2), whereas it has continued to increase in Gulf countries (Saudi Arabia, UAE, Qatar, and Bahrain) and countries with fewer security and political issues (Algeria and Jordan, for example).

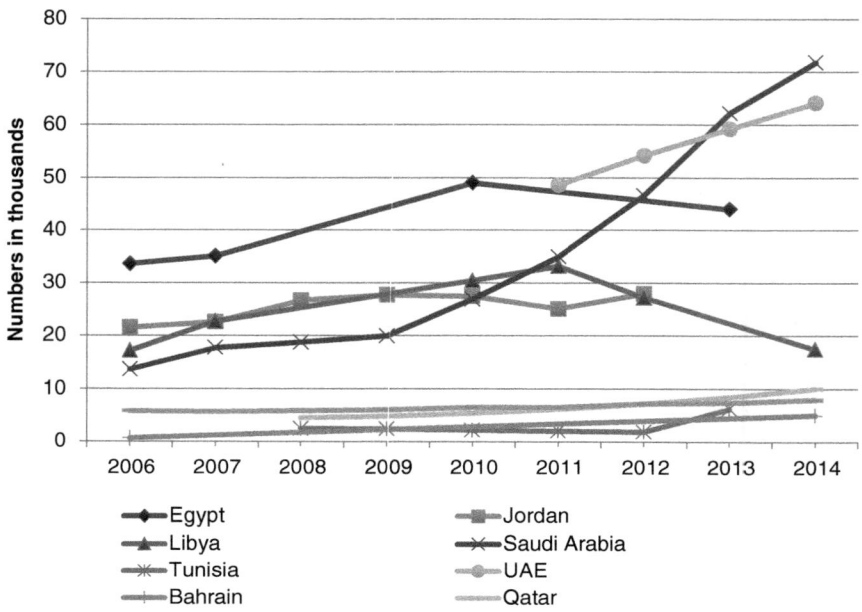

Fig. 2 Total inbound internationally mobile students in selected Arab countries (in thousands)

Note: This graph was generated by Kneoma (http://knoema.fr/WBEDS2016Apr/education-statistics-world-bank-june-2016), based on World Bank Data (June 2016)

In terms of outgoing students, the challenge of internationalizing the HE sector in the Arab world has not yet been met (Fig. 3). In fact, the Arab world accounted for 344,258 students abroad, compared to 1,085,523 from Europe and Central Asia, and 1,168,415 from East Asia and the Pacific regions. In terms of the outbound mobility rate, in 2013 the Arab world recorded annual growth of around 3%, which was higher than other regions with the exception of sub-Saharan Africa. This is explained by the huge demand for HE in the Arab region and the low quality of the local training on offer, which has served to increase the appeal of studying abroad and at international institutions.

However, this increase in Arab students abroad is primarily the result of massive growth in the number of students from Saudi Arabia (from 42,651 in 2010 to 73,548 in 2013). This situation may also be explained

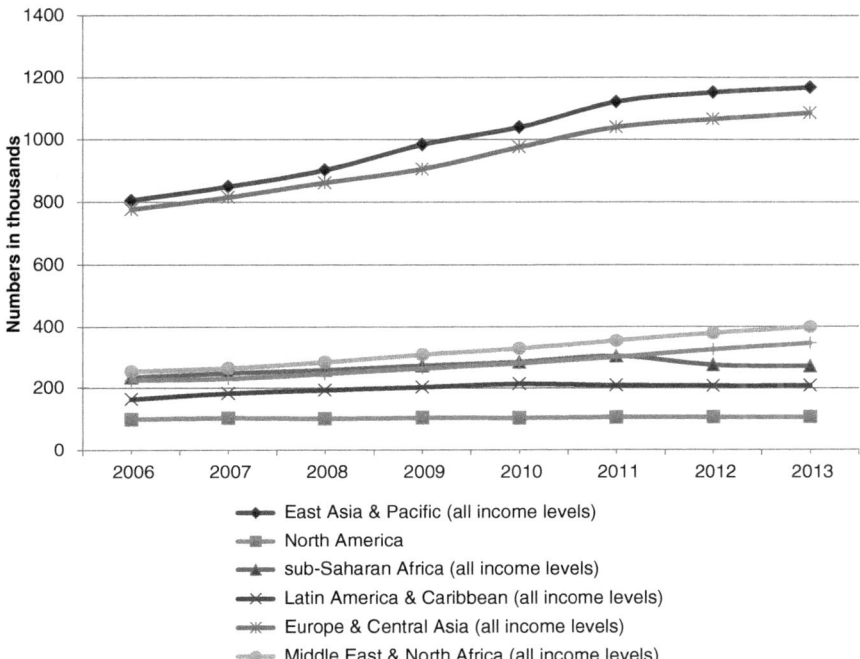

Fig. 3 Total outbound internationally mobile tertiary students studying abroad for all countries, and both sexes (thousands)

Note: This graph was generated by Kneoma (http://knoema.fr/WBEDS2016Apr/educa tion-statistics-world-bank-june-2016), based on World Bank Data (June 2016)

by visa constraints and the cost of international mobility. In addition, the cultural traits of the Arab world may explain why international mobility is less developed in such contexts, in particular when it comes to the international mobility of female students.

Moreover, student mobility in the Arab world relies to a certain degree on inter-Arab student mobility, which limits the cultural diversification that such mobility should generate in order to foster the development of a global culture among Arab students. In 2013, 30% of mobility students in the Arab world came from the region. However, the member countries of the Gulf Cooperation

Council (GCC),[4] and Saudi Arabia and the UAE in particular, attract the great majority of internationally mobile Arab students, ahead of the two traditional destinations for such students, that is, the UK and France. HE in these countries has undergone rapid growth, with an investment of about USD 60 billion during the 2000s (Romani 2012). In 2003, there were only eight universities in Saudi Arabia. Since then, this country alone has created about 100 HE institutions (Mazawi 2004). Other countries, especially UAE and Qatar, have also intensively encouraged the opening of foreign institutions in their territories. For the other Arab countries (Egypt, Lebanon, Jordan, Morocco, Algeria, Syria, Yemen, etc.), Arab students represent a limited percentage of their intake due to the lack of an integrated regional area among the Arab world. In fact, at the political and economic level, the Arab world have limited exchanges. Due to the political conflicts and the huge educational challenges that characterize the region, the Arab world also struggle to foster business transactions between their companies.

Despite this progress in the Gulf states, it would appear that the internationalization of HE in the Arab world has faced a number of obstacles. According to Bhandari and El-Amine (2012), the internationalization of HE in the Arab world is still low in terms of international collaboration and student mobility (incoming and outgoing), especially in public universities, which are the predominant institutions of the HE sector in these contexts. In fact, few Arab HE institutions have a mission statement that encourages the international dimension, and even fewer have an international office and/or campuses outside their home country. The situation is somewhat different in Gulf countries, which are leading the region in terms of internationalization.

To tackle these challenges, we argue that the first thing the Arab world should do is upgrade their local HE sector. They must improve the quality of local education in order to meet the increasing expectations of international and domestic students. HE institutions in the Arab world are still not attractive to international students due to issues of quality. According to the IAU (2014), the Middle East region and Africa

---

[4] The members of the GCC are Saudi Arabia, Qatar, Bahrain, the UAE, Kuwait, Oman, Jordan, and Morocco.

are considered the least attractive for international institutions, and consequently for foreign students. According to the United Nations Development Programme (UNDP, Jāhāna 2015), the satisfaction rate among individuals as regards the quality of education in the Arab world is lower than that recorded in any other region in the world. As a result, 40% of firms in the Arab world state that lack of skills among the labor force is one of the major obstacles to their growth.

In fact, the Arab world have undergone the massification of HE institutions due to demographic changes in these countries. The Arab world has experienced an annual demographic growth rate twice the global average (World Bank 2016). Among the 777 business schools in 52 countries that have earned AACSB accreditation, only 14 are from the Arab world, with four from Saudi Arabia and five from UAE. Furthermore, fewer than 15 Arab universities are ranked among the best 801 universities in the world by the 2015 Times Higher Education ranking.

This strategy of improving the quality of local HE will help the Arab world to avoid, in some cases, the mass departure of their students to other countries. It will also allow the Arab world to meet the expectations of their young people in the wake of the Arab Spring, and consequently improve their social climates. In fact, studying abroad proves a very attractive option for young Moroccans (Chamkhi and Dubois 2011). This is explained by the negative perception people have of their local training programs in the Arab world. Hence there is a need, as stated in the plan, to raise quality standards and to promote international accreditation among local institutions.

The relatively frequent departure of Arab-country students to foreign countries translates into a loss of currency. Above all, it raises the issue of brain drain if one considers the internationalization strategies implemented by some countries, which rely on a search for qualified immigrants that can help check their demographic decline. In Canada, additional waivers are granted to foreign students and work permits are given to HE graduates.

Thus, according to the IAU survey (2014), it appears that the second-highest risk for the African and Middle Eastern region, associated with the internationalization of HE, would be an exodus of talent. This is all the more important when one takes into account the headhunting for talented candidates that now prevails at the international level, which can widen even further the competency gap between developed countries and others. In 2000, the proportion of HE graduates from the Arab world who lived abroad was 8.7%, as opposed to 0.9% in North America, and 5.5% as a world average.

Thus, Arab governments must launch several reforms, increase HE capacities, and implement high-quality standards in their HE institutions. According to El-Amine (2014), Arab governments need to reform their governance systems to allow more financial and administrative autonomy to public institutions, and to reinforce accountability, transparency, and partnerships. Furthermore, they need to increase universities' resources and infrastructures to meet the needs of the increasing numbers of future secondary education graduates. The number of secondary education diploma holders has increased annually by more than 5% in Arab countries, according to the World Bank (2016). This is all the more important when one considers that the number of HE students did not account for more than 27.6% of the population having reached HE in 2013 (World Bank 2016). It is also worth mentioning at this stage that the proportion of the population below 14 years of age in the Arab world is 33%, which is much higher than the world average (World Bank 2016).

Moreover, Arab governments should align the structure of study programs in their HE institutions with internationally recognized ones. For instance, the adoption of ECTS (European Credit Transfer System) or US credits, or an equivalent common system, is essential for student exchange programs. They should also review their policies and regulations to promote, for example, the development of more private institutions and to facilitate the enrollment of international students and the employment of international faculty.

In addition, we suggest courses of action that the Arab world should promote in order to cope with globalization and the internationalization of the HE sector. More specifically, we propose some mechanisms that could be adopted by the Arab world to promote internationalization in their HE sector. We believe that the Arab world must focus on two main strategies: internationalizing home institutions, and attracting international students.

First and foremost, the Arab world must give priority to internationalizing HE at home.

According to this strategy, HE institutions in the Arab world would incorporate global and multicultural dimensions in their various study programs and research activities. It is necessary for local institutions to train graduates who are aware of current international practices in their disciplines and the stakes of globalization. Such a strategy is essential to support the development of the Arab world in a globalized environment, given that the vast majority of students in these countries may not have the opportunity to benefit from an international experience due to costs and visa issues.

To achieve this, several mechanisms may be recommended. First of all, it is possible to create programs focused on specific topics, such as international business, immigration, cross-cultural management, international relations, foreign affairs, and so on. Second, schools may introduce to their existing programs courses that prepare students for the challenges of globalization and for adopting a global vision for their actions. Third, teaching materials (business cases on international companies) and knowledge developed and shared internationally should be taken advantage of. In this respect, it would also be necessary to access international pedagogical resources (data banks, etc.) and employ faculty who are involved in international research projects. For instance, in engineering and medical studies, the teaching must foster the circulation of best practices and techniques developed internationally. This approach to globalizing the curricula is of paramount importance, but it will need to overcome some obstacles. As noted by AACSB (2011), this mechanism will require the support of deans and motivation among the faculty to enrich the content of existing programs and to develop new knowledge on global issues, as well as to build expertise in global issues.

The internationalization of the teaching input may also be achieved by means of learning and assessment activities that encourage students to explore issues linked to globalization and its effects on their environment. For instance, it is worthwhile promoting internships in multicultural environments (e.g., with multinationals), online courses involving foreign faculty and/or students, and online projects with student groups from other countries. Moreover, welcoming foreign visiting faculty and students for short periods may also be useful in bringing diversity to the study environment.

In parallel, the Arab world must encourage intellectual productions on geopolitical, geo-economic, and cross-cultural issues, and comparative studies between countries. Such research is useful to allow decision-makers and experts within the Arab world to decode international signals, anticipate movements and react positively to them, enrich their local practices thanks to international benchmarking, and interact with other cultures in a relevant way. As an example, it is important in management to carry out research on international financial markets, international business techniques, and cross-cultural management in order to develop managerial capability to make business decisions in an international context. Arab HE institutions also need to promote international co-authorships and joint research projects. In doing so, the Arab world will become more attractive to international students and faculty.

Furthermore, to internationalize their contexts, the Arab world should encourage the establishment of international branch campuses and the delivery of dual awards programs within domestic institutions. This can be achieved either by opening international campuses in one or several foreign countries, or by developing partnerships with institutions in the host countries in order to offer a specific program. A report by the British Council and the DAAD (German Academic Exchange Service) (2014) deemed this approach to be one of the most critical in the HE internationalization process. One need only mention that students registered in such offshore programs account for 20% of all students registered in the UK and over 25% of those registered in Australia. In this way, a fair number of students mostly from emerging or developing countries have been able to access international training programs without having to bear the hefty cost of studying abroad and the arduous formalities involved when applying for visas. This is all the more appealing when one considers that international branch campuses and programs imply the presence of foreign faculty members who offer an international experience to local students. In this way, the Arab world could supplement their domestic offers and meet the sizeable needs expressed at the national level.

Such a strategy is also useful for developing an educational hub that is likely to attract the international student population. The best example to date is that of Gulf countries, and more specifically UAE (INSEAD in France, University of Wollongong in Australia, London Business School in the UK, New York University in the USA, etc.), Bahrain (Royal College of Surgeons in Ireland), Kuwait (Maastricht Business School in the Netherlands), Qatar (Cornell University and Carnegie Mellon University in the USA), and Oman (German University of Technology in Germany). These countries have adopted incentive policies for prestigious foreign universities and schools to form regional hubs of excellence. Thus, in the UAE and Qatar, 40 or so foreign university campuses have been set up in a matter of a decade. In Dubai, one can find 26 international campuses from ten different countries (Knowledge and Human Development Authority 2013). In Morocco, between 2014 and 2016, more than five foreign institutions have begun operations (for instance, Ecole Centrale de Casablanca in France).

As regards the second strategy, the Arab world must adopt an international enrollment strategy to attract greater numbers of students.

First, the Arab world must promote, at the regional level, student and faculty exchange programs of short duration. Students often associate such an approach with exchange semesters in a foreign country, which provides them with an international experience as well as validating credits for their home study paths. In this respect, European programs such as ERASMUS and ERASMUS+ are excellent examples of schemes to internationalize training. They offer the possibility for foreign students to have a short-term living and academic experience, and consequently they promote the country as a destination for more extended outbound mobility. To do so, visa constraints between countries in the region have to be reduced and grant programs have to be promoted.

Faculty mobility to carry out research or teaching activities, and to meet professional development needs, is also to be encouraged. Such an approach will bring some international experience to local students, especially in view of the difficulty of recruiting international candidates in some countries due to restrictions and geopolitical issues (terrorism, political instability, etc.).

However, in parallel, the Arab world must also encourage the international recruitment of faculty members, since faculty resources are not yet sufficient. In Morocco, the government will have to recruit some 1,800 lecturers per year until 2020 to compensate for the departures of retirees, and to meet the needs of an increasing number of students. To achieve this, a simplification of the regulations that govern faculty status in Moroccan universities is called for.

Thus, the Arab world could have "global" academic institutions, meaning schools and universities where the learning environment is diversified from a cultural point of view and attractive at the international level. It is indeed necessary nowadays to attract international students and faculty to Arab institutions. In this way, HE systems in the Arab world will be able to share their values with the rest of the world, offer local students a multicultural environment that will help them develop a "global" identity, and, especially, capture the economic and political values of the global flow of internationally mobile students.

In addition, the Arab world must support the emergence of national champions that are able to compete internationally and position themselves at the regional level. To make this happen, authorities in charge of the HE sector in the Arab world must foster the development of university hubs that have sufficient critical mass to enjoy visibility and a good reputation at the international level. In Morocco, a strategy of merging universities into regional clusters was adopted in order to give enhanced visibility to Moroccan universities. The government must also promote international accreditation labels and raise their universities in international rankings.

In doing so, HE institutions in the Arab world will become more appealing to foreign students. This will allow them to recruit more foreign students locally, and to offer their programs on regional campuses for those applicants who cannot travel. Nevertheless, the latter strategy should take heed of two elements. On the one hand, it is important to ensure the quality of the branch campus or the programs deployed abroad in order not to impair the reputation of the country and the institutions. On the other hand, it is advisable to focus on specific programs, for example those aimed at professionals and/or executives who wish to enhance their competencies while employed, in order not to impact the recruitment of regional students locally.

Such an approach may prove very effective in the Arab world given the variety of factors, such as geography, language, and visa issues, that are also at play. For countries such as Morocco, Algeria, Tunisia, and Egypt, sub-Saharan Africa is a very promising market, where the number of households with discretionary income may reach 128 million by 2020, and where training needs are very high, with an estimated 1.1 billion Africans projected to be of working age in 2040 (McKinsey and Company 2010). Likewise, for Gulf countries, where lectures are delivered in English, Asia and the Middle East are markets that offer significant opportunities.

This appears even more important when one considers that students from sub-Saharan Africa and Arab countries have an increasing tendency to favor regional mobility. In fact, according to UNESCO statistics, regional educational hubs are most popular among these students. The percentage of mobile Arab students in the region rose from 12% in 1999 to 30% in 2013. African institutions present their region as the highest-priority destination for the internationalization of their activities. This is very positive for HE institutions in the Arab world, since it will make it easier for them to target students from their regions (Asia or Africa). In fact, the Arab world will find it difficult to attract students from Western countries, compared to those from their region.

Therefore, it appears that the Arab world must pursue an internationalization and globalization process through two strategies: reinforcement of the local training on offer, and regionalization of their HE institutions. These two strategies are essential for countries like those in the Arab world. In fact, due to visa constraints, geopolitical issues, and limited financial resources, these countries need to rely on strong, internationally oriented HE institutions in order to meet local training needs and to meet the expectations of internationally mobile students.

To achieve these two strategies, this chapter has highlighted some mechanisms of internationalization: incorporating the international dimension in local training and research activities, offering dual awards programs through international agreements, opening branches of foreign institutions, reinforcing the local training on offer, supporting the emergence of national and regional champions, and so on. In doing so, according to the World Bank (2011), the Arab world can benefit from the internationalization of their HE by:

- generating more revenue for universities through tuition fees;
- expanding economic impacts for host countries: International students may become a significant source of revenue based on expenditures for transport, housing, tourism, and so on;
- enlarging access to tertiary education: Internationalization of the HE sector has brought additional educational supply;
- increasing the relevance of the tertiary education on offer: The internationalization of Arab HE institutions offers them the opportunity to increase the variety and relevance of their program contents to meet regional challenges, and consequently to enable education to meet the needs of the labor market;
- improving the quality of tertiary education: By internationalizing their HE institutions, the Arab world will encourage them to discover best practices and the relevant resources developed by high-quality institutions;
- strengthening R&D: The internationalization of HE institutions fosters research by enhancing knowledge flows, generating new ideas, developing cooperation in joint research projects, and promoting innovation.

However, these proposed approaches may be applied differently depending on the country's specificities. In fact, some countries, such as the UAE and Saudi Arabia, have already attained the status of regional hubs. In addition, countries like Egypt, Lebanon, Jordan, and Morocco may be better prepared to achieve both strategies at the same time, whereas others (Libya, Yemen, Syria, etc.) may still struggle to achieve any of these approaches due to their political and social situations.

To better understand the situation of each Arab country with regard to the internationalization and globalization of HE, a comprehensive data-collecting exercise is needed to conduct relevant comparative analysis at the national level. In fact, the comparison between regions is sometimes not very precise, since data from some countries are sometimes missing in the aggregate data for a region. It is worth noting as well that the Arab world certainly share Arabic as a language, but they differ at the socioeconomic level. Some countries are influenced by Anglo-Saxon HE systems, while others are more French-culture oriented. There are those with huge oil resources and those without. Given these differences, their internationalization strategies may differ in accordance with their means and challenges. Finally, the analysis of the internationalization of HE in the Arab world must take into account the differences between disciplines. Internationalization appears to be more developed for the management education sector than for other disciplines.

References

AACSB International (2011). *Globalization of Management Education: Changing International Structures, Adaptive Strategies, and the Impact on Institutions.* Report of the AACSB International Globalization of Management Education Task Force. Emerald Group Publishing Limited.

Altbach, P. G., Reisberg, L., and Rumbley, L. E. (2009). *Trends in Global Higher Education: Tracking an Academic Revolution.* A Report Prepared for the UNESCO 2009 World Conference on Higher Education. Paris: UNESCO.

Bhandari, R., and El-Amine, A. (2012). *Higher Education Classification in the Middle East and North Africa: A Pilot Study.* New York (USA): Carnegie Corporation of New York.

British Council and the DAAD (2014). The rationale for sponsoring students to undertake international study: an assessment of national student mobility scholarship programmes. Going Global. United Kingdom.

Chamkhi, A., and Dubois, T. (2011). Étude sur la mobilité internationale des étudiants marocains. Programme EMEMI-AMERM, http://amerm.ma/mim-amerm.

CHE Consult, Brussels Education Services, Centrum für Hochschulentwicklung, Compostela Group of Universities, & Erasmus Student Network (2014). *Erasmus Impact Study. Effects of Mobility on the Skills and Employability of Students and the Internationalization of Higher Education Institutions.* Brussels: European Commission.

Daly, H. (1999). Globalization versus internationalization — some implications. *Ecological Economics*, vol. 31, pp. 31–37.

El-Amine, A. (2014). Quality issues in higher education institutions in Arab countries: A synthesis of case studies. Issues in Higher Education in the Arab Countries (pp. 13–38). Lebanon, Beirut: the Lebanese Association for Educational Studies.

Global Affairs Canada (2012). International Education: A Key Driver of Canada's Future Prosperity. Final Report of the Advisory Panel on Canada's International Education Strategy.

IAU (2014). *Internationalization of Higher Education: Growing Expectations, Fundamental Values* The IAU 4th Global Survey Executive Summary done by Eva Egron-Polak and Ross Hudson.

IMF (2008). *Globalization: A Brief Overview*. https://www.imf.org/external/np/exr/ib/2008/053008.htm (Accessed on January 2017).

IMF (2016). *The Role of Emerging Markets in a New Global Partnership for Growth*. Speech of IMF Managing Director Christine Lagarde at the University of Maryland, February 4, 2016 (https://www.imf.org/en/News/Articles/2015/09/28/04/53/sp020416#P26_3020).

Iniguez, S. (2012). Sources of income and internationalization of Business Schools. Presentation made at the European University Association (EUA) Funding Forum in Salzburg The text has been adapted from the author's book *The Learning Curve: How Business Schools Are Reinventing Higher Education* (London: Palgrave Macmillan, 2011).

Institute of Higher Education (2015). *IE Releases Open Doors 2015 Data*.

Jāhāna, S. (2015). *Human development report 2015: Work for human development*. United Nations Development Programme.

Knight, J. (2008). *Higher Education in Turmoil. The Changing World of Internationalization*. Rotterdam: Sense Publishers.

Knowledge and Human Development Authority (2013). The Higher Education Landscape in Dubai 2012. (https://www.khda.gov.ae/hesummit/pdf/HELandscape2012.pdf). Accessed on January 2017.

Mazawi, André (2004). "War, geopolitics and university governance in the Arab states". *International Higher Education*, vol. 36, pp. 7–9.

McKinsey and Company (2010). *Lions on the Move: The Progress and Potential of African Economies*. United Kingdom: McKinsey Global Institute.

OECD (2010). *Measuring Globalization: OECD Economic Globalization Indicators 2010*. Paris (France): OCDE.

Romani, V. (2012). Internationalisation des politiques universitaires et contournement de leurs publics? *Revue des Mondes musulmans et de la Méditerranée*, vol. 131 (June 2012), pp. 13–21.

UNESCO Institute for Lifelong Learning (UIL) (2014). *Medium-term Strategy 2014–2021: Laying Foundations for Equitable Lifelong Learning For All.*

World Bank (2011). *Internationalization of Higher Education in MENA: Policy Issues Associated with Skills Formation and Mobility.* Washington, DC.

World Bank (2016). *World Bank Development Indicators Database. World Databank.* Washington, DC. http://data.worldbank.org. Consulted in August 2016.

Imad-eddine Hatimi holds a Ph.D. in Business Administration (Strategy & Innovation) and a Master's in Management from HEC Montréal as well as a Master's in Applied Sciences (Civil Engineering) from Sherbrooke University in Canada. His research has focused on innovation in management and new institutional theories. In 2004, jointly with Taïeb Hasfi, he was awarded the Best Article Prize by the Canadian Journal of Administrative Sciences. In Canada, he was a research assistant and lecturer at HEC Montréal and a consultant in Strategic Management, Organisational Development and human resource management for various firms. Since his return to Morocco, he has been the Dean of the Faculty of Management at Mundiapolis University (2008–2011) and the Associate Dean in charge of Accreditations at ESCA Ecole de Management (since 2012).

"Zero-Based" Governance: A New Model for the Future

Nabil A. Husni

Introduction

Governance of higher education (HE) has been changing and evolving all around the world. The Arab world is going through a multidimensional revolution in areas related to educational, economic, and political development. The 2002 United Nations Development Programme's Arab Human Development Report identified education as a major force for increasing the rate of change and progress. The report identified three areas in need of major reform: enhancing human capabilities, creating synergy between education and the socioeconomic system, and developing a plan for education reform. A 2012 pilot study conducted by Bhandari and El-Amine and supported by the Carnegie Corporation of New York indicated that the lack of a common framework for HE in the Arab world has major negative implications for stakeholders at many levels, including research, organizational structure,

N.A. Husni (✉)
Adma International School, Middle East, Lebanon
e-mail: nabilhusni127@gmail.com

© The Author(s) 2018
G. Azzi (ed.), *Higher Education Governance in the Arab World*,
DOI 10.1007/978-3-319-52060-5_3

selection of majors, policymaking, and industry. Most HE institutions (HEIs) are aligned with an international model of education. The cultural orientation of each institution depends on its historical affiliation, language, and curriculum and on the nature of its governance. The most dominant models of HEIs in the Arab region are the French and American models. Key challenges to meaningful reform in governance of HE include the following:

- lack of a learner-centered educational philosophy in most K through 16 educational organizations;
- persistence of a traditional understanding and implementation of leadership;
- negative perceptions of vocational education;
- the decline in quality due to the rapid growth of new colleges and universities and increases in enrollment within many HEIs;
- the small degree of autonomy at most HEIs;
- the need for extensive funding to keep up with rapid change and development;
- lack of political and economic stability in most countries of the Arab world;
- lack of shared governance within governments of the Arab world;
- the narrow and limiting definition of the role of HEIs in society;
- limiting or eliminating the role of many stakeholders in the governance of HEIs;
- the absence of reliable and standardized institutional-level data in relation to HEIs on development and governance within the Arab world.

It will be impossible to overcome these challenges if we continue to utilize existing leadership and governance models. On the other hand, it will be difficult but feasible to overcome them if we adopt a holistic leadership and educational philosophy and a new model for governance. It is a long process that involves reforming the political systems and the K through 16 educational institutions by promoting democracy, social justice, conflict resolution, and human rights.

History of HE in the Arab World

Before exploring the different avenues of reform and new models of governance, we should understand the history of the development of HE in the Arab world.

"Higher learning is deeply rooted in the history and societies of the Arab Middle East. After the seventh century and the Islamization of the Arab world, local religious schools known as madrasa became the main institutions of higher learning in the Middle East. They established and disseminated educational standards that are still applied in present-day universities, such as the separation of Master's from doctorate programs, tenure, and protections for academic freedom. Madrasas such as al-Azhar in Cairo and the Qarawiyyun in Fez originated in intellectual movements such as humanism and scholasticism, which nurtured the subsequent flourishing of Western scholarship after the twelfth century.

During the same period, other institutions of the Arab world, such as hospitals, libraries, observatories, and private homes known as 'academies' undertook the development of the nonreligious sciences, inspired by the ancient Greeks. The most famous of these academies was the Beit al Hikma (House of Wisdom) in Baghdad, where numerous fields within the sciences (astronomy, physics, mathematics, medicine, chemistry, geography) flourished until the sixteenth century. By the dawn of the Italian Renaissance, the knowledge cultivated within these disciplines and others had been translated and transmitted to Europe through Italy and Spain.

As dominance over the Mediterranean shifted to Europe after the sixteenth century—only to increase during the Renaissance and, subsequently, the Industrial Revolution—the place of the Arab Middle East in the academic world underwent a dramatic reversal. Yet the Ottomans, who ruled the Arab world throughout this period, strove as early as the eighteenth century to get their Empire back into the academic game. In 1720, the Sultan Ahmet III sent delegations of scholars to Europe in order to obtain translations of Western scientific books. This pattern reached its peak during the reign of Mohamed Ali (r. 1805–1849), when dozens of modern institutions of higher learning were established on the European model, mainly in

Egypt. Meanwhile—in fact, since the eighteenth century—European missionaries, followed by American Christians, were founding dozens of schools and institutions of higher learning in the Middle East, while the French established institutions of higher learning in North Africa; thus, neither the globalization of higher education nor 'Westernization' is a new trend in the Middle East" (Romani 2009, pp. 2–3).

Discussing the Arab world as a whole is itself a complex undertaking. Approximately 36% of all HEIs are private in nature, while private sector universities represent more than 80% of all universities in Bahrain, Lebanon, Palestine, Qatar, and the United Arab Emirates. On the other hand, private universities comprise fewer than 20% of the total in Algeria, Iraq, Libya, and Morocco (Wilkens 2011). Lebanon's HE is the oldest in the region. It started in 1866, when the American University of Beirut (AUB) was established as the Syrian Evangelical College. This was followed by the University of Saint Joseph (USJ) in 1875. Since that time, many other universities have been founded. The biggest increase came in the 1990s, following the end of the civil war, which lasted from 1975 until 1990. Currently, Lebanon has 42 HEIs, which are divided into two categories: vocational tertiary education and general higher education. According to a document produced by the National Tempus Office of Lebanon in 2012, the governing bodies of the HEIs of Lebanese private and public universities are formulated in a similar manner.

> The Lebanese university is a large, centralized institution headed by a president and governed by a university council in which each faculty is represented by its dean and one academic elected by the teaching staff. Students and the government each also have two representatives on this council. In addition, the council includes three independent qualified experts chosen by the government. The president, with the council of the university and through the deans of the faculties, has a great deal of authority in the management of the university (Al Soufi and Jammal 2012, p. 4).

As for the private sector, each HEI is required by law to have a board of trustees, two-thirds of whom must not be related to the owners.

Unfortunately, many stakeholders are not represented in governance. Additionally, religiously funded institutions have their own governance systems, which correlate with their internal mechanisms.

As for the Middle East and North Africa (MENA) countries, they had only ten universities in 1940, 140 HEIs in 2000, and 260 in 2007 (Romani 2009). The number of universities reached 398 in 2011 (Wilkens 2011). It must be noted that community colleges, teacher training institutes, and technical institutions are not included in these numbers. Unlike the early model introduced by American missionaries, the new foreign universities and HEIs affiliated with foreign universities are for-profit institutions. There has been a dramatic increase in universities associated with Western countries and foreign branch campuses, in particular in the United Arab Emirates and Qatar (Lasanowski 2010). These universities have diverse programs and curricula that cater for both students of the host countries and international students. However, this development is not valid for most of the non-Gulf countries, and the quality of most Arabic HEIs may not have kept pace with international standards. This dramatic expansion in the Gulf countries is associated with several factors: first, the poor performance of state universities that were founded in the 1960s after the Gulf countries secured their independence (Ghabra and Arnold 2007); second, the fact that between 25% and 75% of the population of the Gulf countries are foreign expatriates (Willoughby 2008); third, the need for knowledge-based societies to sustain post-oil economies; and finally, the preference among Arab students to remain in their home countries in view of the security constraints imposed upon them after the September 11, 2001 attacks on the USA. These constraints are expected to increase as a result of the current wave of violence by extremist groups operating under different Islamic names, despite their lack of representation of or resemblance to true Islamic values.

The huge discrepancies among countries in the Arab world will have severe consequences for countries such as Egypt and Algeria. The social, political, and economic crisis in Egypt resulting from the loss of competitiveness of its HEIs is forcing students to seek education outside the country; similarly, Algeria, which exports half a million members of its workforce, mostly to Europe, is heading toward a disastrous situation.

The Gulf countries' aim to be a hub for economic and educational development promises to be a great asset for these countries, but may serve as a huge threat to the remainder of the Arab world. The challenge for the Arab world, including the Gulf states, is to develop multidimensional universities that promote educational excellence, support economic vitality, advance peace education (democracy and citizenship, human rights, conflict resolution, environmental education, health and safety, and service learning), endorse meaningful and holistic leadership, and support a well-defined and comprehensive shared governance model.

Governance and the Purpose of Higher Education

Governance has been defined in many ways over the years. Arguably, the three key elements for good governance are accountability, transparency, and decision-making processes. Governance can be defined as the process by which an organization conducts assessments and evaluations and makes decisions and implements them, and how the stakeholders relate to each other, to the organization, and to society at large. In order to explore new models of governance based on this definition, we must raise the following questions: Who is a stakeholder? Who are the stakeholders of a university? How and why has the role of governance changed over time? Should students play a role in governance? What is the purpose of HE? How do we ensure that students play an effective role in governance? Should external stakeholders be represented on the board of trustees? What are the roles of different governments?

We will explore different views on HE and its governance in order to directly or indirectly answer these questions and pave the way to developing a new governance model.

The Chair of the Council's Higher Education and Research Committee (CD-ESR) pilot project on the University as a Site of Citizenship identified several issues in which HEIs have a role to play. The issues include internal academic and non-academic mechanisms and decision-making within the institution itself, the institution as a multicultural society, and the institution's relationship and interaction with the wider society (Oslo, June 12–14, 2003).

The purposes of HE include "preparation for the labor market, preparation for life as active citizens in a democratic society, personal development, and development and maintenance of an advanced knowledge base" (Bergan 2003, p. 11).

As the purpose of HE continues to evolve, so too does the need to find a common definition of governance. The following set of definitions includes those offered by various scholars since the concept was introduced in 1920.

(1) It is a "social system of self-government wherein decision-making responsibility is shared among those affected by the decisions" (Lau 1996).

(2) Shared governance is a "system of governance whereby the decision-making capacity of the institution is shared by those affected by the decisions; these include the boards, administrators, faculty, staff and students" (Schuetz 1999).

(3) Shared governance can be thought of as a "sharing of responsibility by faculty, administration, staff, appointed personnel and students, for making decisions about institutional missions, policies and budget priorities" (University of Arizona 2003).

(4) Shared governance "reflects the view that colleges and universities ought to be run by their most immediate stakeholders, primarily by faculty, professional staff, and students" (Trakman 2008).

(5) Ben-Ruwin introduced in 2010 a new shared governance model that he called the "satisfactory shared governance model." He argued that consensual, participatory, accountable, transparent, responsive, communicative, efficient, and equitable are eight characteristics that are essential in order for a shared governance model to be satisfactory. Furthermore, he stated that "Academic Freedom, Shared Vision, and Collective Trust" are the three prerequisite values that are essential for the success of a shared governance model. He concluded his study by endorsing shared governance as a viable model and pointing out that there is no model that fits all educational institutions.

> The concept of shared governance in academe is facing major challenges from internal and external forces attempting to replace it with a corporate managerial model. Thus the question facing academe today is: What should [be] the response by faculty to these perceived anti-intellectual elites that try to corporatize the concept of shared governance by implementing the business's managerial model? (Ben-Ruwin 2010, p. 2).

The struggle continues between advocates of the business model, who believe that profit is the main goal and that economic vitality is within its vision, and the shared governance model, which focuses on maintaining the integrity of the institution and preventing the pressure of commercialization from distorting its mission. Unfortunately, with the current realities of the economic situation, governmental regulations, and the existing political systems, we cannot view governance as a dichotomy according to which it is seen as an either/or situation. In order to close the gap between the two models, we must revisit learner-centered education inclusive of peace education and holistic leadership from K through 16. Advancing these ideas will make it easier for individuals from diverse backgrounds to find a common vision for building and/or accepting a new model of shared governance. In essence, we need to transform our educational systems instead of reforming them.

Transforming Our Educational Systems

Despite the billions of dollars spent on many initiatives over the last three decades, meaningful educational reform remains elusive. It is sad to think that Winston Churchill's statement "The only time my education was interrupted was while I was at school" still holds true today.

Most educators, if not all, talk about how they would like to see each one of our graduates become an empathetic human being, a good communicator, a celebrator of diversity, a critical thinker, an endorser of peace education, a problem-solver, a creative researcher, a team player, an effective leader, a technology expert, a positive change agent, a self-reflector, an innovative risk taker, an independent learner, and an academic achiever. They may also recognize that effective teachers must inspire students to become self-motivated and support them in learning; communicate through active, empathetic listening; engage in continuous self-evaluation; utilize differentiated learning to accommodate diverse learning styles and multiple intelligences, needs, and gifts; promote integrated and active learning through the use of interactive technology; endorse authentic assessment and use it to promote learning; facilitate all aspects of the learning process with passion; embody a holistic approach to education; manage their class effectively; set high expectations for each student; recognize student success at every step; promote partnerships with parents; celebrate diversity; embrace peace education through democracy and citizenship, conflict resolution, human rights, health and safety, environmental education, and service learning; and be intrinsically motivated. However, the reality shows that most graduates are ill-prepared to face the challenges of a rapidly changing world and that most teachers are far from effective. You may ask, what went wrong?

Unfortunately, despite well-intended reform, the educational community must realize that even the most meaningful reform is no longer sufficient. We must switch from educational reform to educational transformation. We must transform schools and universities from teacher-centered institutions that transfer knowledge to learner-centered organizations that provide an environment that is supportive of the learning process. Just as Edison invented the light bulb instead of adding more candles, we must revisit the idea of teaching and learning and creatively redefine its purpose. It must be apparent that we can no longer keep adjusting rigid curricula that focus on what to teach. Instead, we must transform each curriculum into a document that focuses on learning objectives and how meaningful learning is measured through authentic assessment, and that endorses inquiry learning and higher-order thinking—in short, a document that promotes holistic development through integrated, cooperative, and differentiated learning.

Transforming education is about creating an environment that enhances the ability of learners to be empathetic and gives them the motivation and interest to think and learn. It is about engaging learners in self-reflection and enabling them to know how to take risks, have fun, be creative, and be aware of and manage emotions. It is about kindling learners' curiosity, courage, and imagination, in addition to sharpening their communication, social, and leadership skills.

Simply put, the process of reform sets high expectations of learners without providing them with the means to achieve them. This uneven equation makes learners insecure, adds negative stress to their lives, and decreases their rate of success.

In order to meet the high expectations we have of our learners, in particular students and teachers, we must transform the entire institution to become an effective, innovative, and learner-centered organization. Such an organization necessitates the presence of the following documents, concepts, and characteristics:

1. a strategic plan;
2. common and shared vision;
3. leadership density;
4. readiness for change;
5. effective leadership;
6. a learner-centered approach to education;
7. continuous professional development;
8. holistic development of the child: social, emotional, moral, spiritual, academic, and cognitive;
9. holistic and diverse curriculum inclusive of peace education and integrated learning, and reflective of the culture;
10. diverse teaching and learning strategies inclusive of cooperative and inquiry learning leading to better retention and higher-order thinking;
11. use of technology to promote networking, partnership, and integrated and differentiated learning;
12. continuous formative and summative traditional and authentic assessment that is linked to teaching, learning, and professional development, and is reflective of the organization's mission;
13. involvement of the entire organization constituency in the planning and implementation stages (students, staff members, teachers, administrators, parents, board of trustees, and community members);
14. educated parents who have high expectations of their children and who encourage them to explore and use an active problem-solving approach to resolve conflict;
15. financial stability and a budget that is linked to the strategic plan;

16. highly qualified teachers, administrators, and staff members;
17. visionary board of trustees that encompasses all stakeholders and supports the administration but does not interfere with the daily operation of the organization. Students of such organizations develop higher-order thinking skills, have better communication and social skills, can apply knowledge to real-life situations, become intrinsically and morally motivated, build confidence and self-esteem, are aware of rights and responsibilities, support social justice, become positive change agents, and endorse peace education as a way of life. Only these kinds of students can become active stakeholders and effective members within the governing process.

Peace Education

Peace education is known internationally by many names, including moral education, values-based education, and character education, among others. Each variant has a slightly different meaning, pointing to one or other distinctive emphasis. However, all these variants have in common the belief that personal, social, and spiritual development based on a "glocal" set of values must be at the heart of a learner-centered education.

A holistic and integrated approach to peace education leading to positive human development has been endorsed and supported by universal declarations, global and regional pronouncements and commitments, and other documents, which share a belief in the importance of values in a holistic and integrated education that aims toward a culture of peace and social justice, among them:

1. The Universal Declaration of Human Rights (United Nations [UN], 1948), Article 26(2), which states that: "Education shall be directed to the full development of the human personality and to the strengthening of respect for human rights and fundamental freedoms. It shall promote understanding, tolerance and friendship among all nations, racial or religious groups, and shall further the activities of the United Nations for the maintenance of peace."

2. The UN Declaration on a Culture of Peace (UN 1999), which states that: "Progress in the development of a culture of peace comes through values, attitudes, modes of behavior and ways of life conducive to the promotion of peace among individuals, groups and nations." The declaration also recommends that a culture of peace be fostered through education by "ensuring that children benefit from education on the values, attitudes, modes of behavior and ways of life enabling them to resolve disputes peacefully . . . instilling in them the values and goals of a culture of peace."

3. The 1993 Kuala Lumpur Declaration of the Ministers of Education of the Asia-Pacific Region (MINEDAP V1), which states that their overarching concern was the importance of values, ethics, and culture in education.

4. The United Nations Educational, Scientific, and Cultural Organization (UNESCO) 21st Century Talks (UNESCO), in which the role of values and ethics in ensuring a peaceful and sustainable future is frequently emphasized. Universal values and ethics are here described as "the companion of knowledge and wisdom . . . a concept which is both multi-dimensional and multi-disciplinary . . . and of vital importance to the world."

5. The Character Education Handbook and Guide in North Carolina, USA, 2001 (Public Schools of North Carolina 2001).

6. The Character and Citizenship Education in Alberta Schools, Canada, 2006.

7. Citizenship Education in Europe, 2012.

8. The Manifesto on Values, Education, and Democracy—Department of Education of South Africa 2001.

9. The Melbourne Declaration on Educational Goals for Young Australians, 2008.

10. The Shape of the Australian Curriculum, 2011.

Peace education goes beyond the absence of war; it is a way of life. It is a complete transformation of thoughts, values, skills, actions, and eventually habits. Arguably, the three major factors responsible for the continuous violence throughout history are the attempt to resist violence by using violence, being passive about promoting peace education, and endorsing an educational system that is authority-centered. If history teaches us anything at all, it clearly shows that violence produces more violence. It also teaches us that lighting candles, holding hands, and chanting love songs are positive acts, but are not sufficient to overcome aggression and stop wars. Additionally, it has become clear that we must switch all educational organizations from "authority-centered" to "learner-centered" environments (Husni 2015, pp. 86–87).

The components of peace education include democracy and citizenship, human rights, conflict resolution, environmental education, health and safety, and service learning.

The ability to move into a learner-centered philosophy inclusive of peace education and toward a comprehensive shared governance model requires effective leadership. The following summary of effective leadership and its characteristics is from the book *Leadership and Holistic Education* (Husni 2015).

Leadership

Leadership is about doing the right thing. It is motivating, enabling, and empowering others to do their best while learning from them. It is the ability to respond to change in a positive and constructive manner. It is knowing that there is a solution for every problem and that we always have a choice in how we respond to people's words and actions. What matters is what you do; promises are meaningless. Leadership is about modeling your philosophy through your actions.

Values that allow us to exercise effective leadership, implement our philosophy, enjoy the process, celebrate success, and achieve results include but are not limited to the following:

- faith gives us power;
- goodness gives us confidence;
- giving gives us joy;
- forgiveness gives us serenity;
- gratitude gives us freedom;

- courage gives us uniqueness;
- positive thinking gives us a head start;
- self-management, self-control, and effective communication skills give us flexibility;
- perseverance gives us continuity;
- empathy gives us humanity;
- passion gives us energy.

Leadership fails when our actions are inconsistent with our words and when we abuse our power. Remember, reputation is what others know about you. Honor is what you know about yourself.

Characteristics, Skills, and Concepts Essential for Effective Leadership

The greatest myth of all is the belief that a person needs permission or has to be in charge in order to be a leader. Leadership is learned, and the key ingredients that are needed are already within you. It is time to begin the transformation process to becoming the leader you can and always wanted to be. The following guidelines may be helpful in speeding up the process (Taylor 2003).

Believing You Can Be a Leader

Leadership is a skill and a habit. Like most skills and habits, leadership improves with practice. As you become more skilled, the habit takes over and you begin to worry less about the mechanics of doing it and focus more on achieving your goals. Leaders are leaders because they have self-confidence and a commitment to making a difference in whatever capacity possible (Burchard 2012). Making your positive thoughts a reality requires the ability to visualize, persevere, and act with passion. Only then does your behavior become different, and over time it transfers into habits that are stored in the subconscious mind. You can store as many new habits as you desire. Doing so gives you a wealth of resources at your fingertips to begin your journey of leadership (Bryne 2006). Get ready! An exciting journey is ahead of you. Begin now and act as if you have arrived, instead of thinking "I will make it happen soon."

Effective Communication

The secret is to get your message across and learn how to listen. With good communication skills, you can expect to express your thoughts, mediate, educate, inform, learn, and even inspire. This is why communication is the driving force behind effective leadership. Remember, communication is a two-way street. When one party is sending a message, the other party should receive it in the way it was meant. As a leader, you should develop positive and active listening skills. This gives the people working with you a feeling of comfort. They know they can come to you with problems, ideas, or initiatives, convinced that you will listen and respond to the message they are sending. Communicating your desire to lead will open doors for you and allow you to exercise leadership in many different ways over and over again. The following is a list of helpful reminders that will improve your communication skills:

As you listen:

- focus totally on the person you are listening to;
- use body language to reinforce your interest in what is being said;
- express that you have understood the emotional impact;
- do not interrupt, unless to indicate interest in a specific area or to seek further clarification;
- be ready to repeat what the other person has said using feeling language;
- allow the speaker to confirm or contradict your understanding of what he/she has said.

As you talk:

- stay aware of your emotions;
- ensure control of your emotions;

- speak with confidence and project;
- use the right language in relation to your audience;
- use your eyes and maintain the right body posture;
- make it real and simple—avoid jargon;
- gather clues from the listener's body language and emotional state;
- do your homework—be prepared and learn to pause, think, and then respond.

Active and positive listening have two ingredients: empathy and acceptance. Empathy is the ability to understand others' views of reality even though they may differ from ours, in addition to being able to identify and understand others' feelings. Acceptance is the ability to take another person's position as true for them irrespective of any agreement. Active listening is one of the critical skills needed to be an effective problem-solver and an effective communicator. Another benefit of good communication skills is the ability to facilitate a dialogue. Dialogue is a method to help solve problems and manage differences.

Becoming "Change Ready"

The paradox created by the two statements, "Change is the only constant" and "The more things change, the more they remain the same," is what makes being "change ready" intriguing, interesting, challenging, difficult, and worrisome, but also possible given the right environment, the willingness to adopt a new set of values, and the courage to do so. The fact that change is a process or a journey, and not a result or destination, makes it difficult to accept. We tend to view change as a total, discrete event. As such, people think either they can change something or somebody or they cannot. In order to accept the feasibility of change, we must view it as a continuum made up of many parts, and when one part does not change, it is not an indication that the other parts will not or cannot do so (Adams 2001). Therefore, we should not generalize; we must be specific, patient, and persevering, and we should celebrate each small change or success as a total victory and hence live in and celebrate the present. Although the environment plays a key role in shaping who we are, we also have genetic characteristics that affect our personalities, and these characteristics are very difficult, if not impossible, to change permanently. However, we can, at least, enhance any and all characteristics in order to reach an acceptable functioning level. We may change one thing at a time and celebrate it, remembering that change is situational and that it is feasible to change most or all the parts immediately or at a later time. The key is the timing of the change. Sometimes we make the change too quickly, and other times we wait too long and miss the boat. Do not forget that it is a journey with many stations, and you must adapt and enjoy every station regardless of when and how the journey will end. Live in the present and make your station and/or your vocation a vacation.

The simplest way to change is to assume that change has already occurred and act accordingly, instead of saying, "I will make the change." Assuming the change has already occurred is utilizing positive thinking, which can be transformed into a new habit through visualization, perseverance, and consistent, passionate action.

These new habits will be stored in the subconscious mind and become the new reality. The challenge is to eliminate all doubt about the occurrence of change from the subconscious mind. Simply put, you are capable of changing immediately. The choice is yours. However, do not forget that choosing not to change, or to change again, are among your options.

Motivation

Bruce and Pepitone (1999) believed that we can motivate people to do their best, take pride in what they do, and accomplish better results for an organization by using:

1. positive feedback: Effective feedback statements should be job- or task-oriented, specific, timely, personal, and most importantly genuine;
2. an inclusionary approach: A process that builds a collaborative or partnership environment encourages all participants to play leadership roles in order to feel a sense of ownership;

3. constructive criticism: Ignoring mistakes or shortcomings of people, even ones who are among the most productive members of the organization, hinders the growth of these individuals, causes morale issues, and prevents the organization from reaching new heights. As in the case of positive feedback, criticism should be positive, timely, and specific. It should also be non-threatening and serve as a learning opportunity.

Tangible rewards, such as pay increases and advancement, are useful and motivating in the short term. However, they quickly lose their meaning as they become part of the system and expected by everybody. Rewards with lasting impact must be more personal and unique. We should focus on intangible rewards that are more intrinsic or moral in nature. As such, the focus should continue to be on empowerment, inclusion, and leadership density.

Many psychologists believe that our actions are motivated by needs. Maslow's (1954) "hierarchy of needs" classifies needs into essential and non-essential. It is typically represented by a pyramid, with basic needs at the bottom. The following is a summary of the different needs represented by the pyramid:

1. Basic needs include the elements for survival, such as the need to breathe, eat, drink, sleep, and reproduce.
2. Safety needs are about feeling safe. They include the need to be sheltered from the elements and to be free from danger and fear.
3. Social needs are about having a sense of belonging. They include the need to find affection and acceptance among family, friends, and others.
4. Esteem needs are related to feeling proud of our accomplishments. They include the need to feel valued and respected.
5. Self-actualization needs are about making full use of our abilities and finding our true purpose in life.
6. Self-transcendence needs are about doing things higher than ourselves.

In essence, what motivates a human being changes, since our needs, interests, and what makes us feel good vary with time, place, and situation. Therefore, you should utilize diverse motivational tools and strategies that correlate with timely assessments of each member of the team.

Empowerment and Team Building

Empowerment is a departure from viewing the organization as a combination of several discrete elements, where challenges and problems are treated as a series of causes and effects. It is about acknowledging that all elements of the system are intertwined. It is about sharing all information with all members of the school and delegating decision-making to the people closest to the core worker and clients. It means endorsing participatory management and shared leadership.

The endorsement of openness, trust, loyalty, and happiness combined with a sincere and serious effort to encourage and develop people through coaching and support will promote involvement, real empowerment, and personal growth by strengthening people's inner belief systems and self-confidence. Endorsing this concept leads to motivated, able, committed, and competent people working interdependently in an open and supportive environment. Congratulations, you have developed and endorsed teamwork as a way of doing business, which will make your organization a happier and more productive place.

Conflict Resolution

The best way to resolve conflict is to have an open, motivating, and supportive atmosphere whereby conflict is eliminated before it even starts. Unfortunately, being human translates into making mistakes, which will lead to conflicts between and among individuals. The fact that we are not all on the same page, or on the same path, makes it difficult for people to understand and accept other people's positions (Adams 2001). Additionally, differences in personalities, values, and attitudes are also sources that invite conflict. The following is a set of suggestions that are helpful in resolving conflicts:

1. Use a problem-solving approach by listening to everybody involved. Then, agree on a decision that minimizes losses for the different individuals and enhances the chance of a win–win situation when feasible.
2. Utilize good organizational and time management skills. Learn to prioritize your goals and set an action plan to achieve them. This will keep you focused and reduce stress, which minimizes conflict and enables you to deal with it if and when it occurs in the future.
3. Ensure that everybody has a sense of ownership of the strategic plan. People with a common vision, mission, values, and goals are more likely to see differences as a chance to improve instead of as a major conflict. They also begin to view issues in a similar way.
4. Help each member of the organization enhance the skills needed to ensure a highly functioning emotional intelligence (EQ). In other words, mastering the skills and/or values of self-awareness, self-discipline, empathy, perseverance, and social interaction are of utmost importance in helping us deal with conflict.
5. Promote third-option thinking, which leads to synergy and makes a win–win situation the most likely outcome. Third-option thinking implies that both parties believe they can reach an alternative solution that is different from either party's solution. It encourages each party to seek out the other because they have different views. It produces exponential growth in solutions. It may even make $1 + 1 = 1,000$ (Covey 2011).

Learning from Mistakes

As the saying goes, successful people learn from their own mistakes, while people who excel learn from their own mistakes and the mistakes of others. We must remember that mistakes are learning opportunities. In each mistake, there is a valuable lesson to be learned, a chance to change and improve matters. The main issue is to make the proper plans to ensure that the same mistake is not repeated. Effective leaders do not dwell on mistakes or get stuck in the past. They embrace the present and move forward (Tozer 2012).

Professional Development, Assessment, and Evaluation

Targeted professional development is crucial to continuous improvement of the organization and to the personal and professional growth of each of its members. A comprehensive evaluation plan (ongoing, informal, formal, formative, and summative) should be inclusive of everyone (board of trustees, administrators, teachers, staff members, workers, and students). You should develop a comprehensive plan for professional development that is based on the following premises:

1. enhancing the learning process, which is the main reason for assessment;
2. promoting the vision and endorsing the mission and values of the organization;
3. establishing an incentive program that correlates with the summative evaluation;
4. achieving the goals of the organization;
5. meeting the needs of each member of the organization as identified by the continuous assessment and evaluation procedures;
6. giving each member the opportunity to be a leader;
7. using a portfolio system that utilizes student, teacher, administrator, and self-input.

Volunteerism

Giving back to the community can be a great opportunity to ignite your passion, to feel better, and to enhance your leadership skills. It also reinforces the value of commitment and perseverance. It is peace education in action and is an important part of becoming a holistic leader.

Recruitment and Retention of Employees

This is an area that requires a lot of change. We must move from thinking that one or a few people are responsible for recruitment and retention to believing that it is the responsibility of every person. This may be one of the most important decisions we make. Bringing new, quality people to an organization and ensuring continuity are of utmost importance. The following are essential steps to managing the success of these procedures:

1. Recruitment:

   • Set special criteria for new candidates.

   Do a background check:

   • Invite your employees to nominate people to fill vacancies.
   • Develop and train hiring committees.
   • Set a process for making final decisions.

2. Retention:

   • Conduct an orientation session with follow-up, workshops, and evaluation.
   • Articulate clear expectations.
   • Assign a mentor for each new person.
   • Provide a supportive atmosphere and recognize achievement regularly.
   • Develop an incentive plan that promotes a combination of extrinsic, intrinsic, and moral motivators.

Being Visible

It has been said that "A picture is worth a thousand words." I say your presence is priceless. Being visible and available, especially when your presence is not planned, expected, or scheduled, is meaningful and rewarding. The following ideas are useful in helping you to become more visible and/or available:

1. Walk around, relate, and interact with visitors, teachers, students, administrators, and workers.
2. Walk around campus when classes are in session.
3. Visit classes for five minutes or a whole period.
4. Have your snack in the faculty lounge.

Agility in Leadership Style

An effective leader is capable of wearing many hats and able to adjust his/her style to suit diverse situations. This implies that you are able to utilize the theory of situational leadership (Blanchard et al. 2013). It means assessing a teacher's or an administrator's competence in and commitment to a specific objective or task and having the ability to:

1. delegate to individuals with high competence and high commitment;
2. support individuals with moderate to high competence and variable commitment;
3. coach individuals with low to some competence and low commitment;
4. direct individuals with low competence and high commitment.

In essence, you should adjust your style on a regular basis, even with the same individual, since competence and commitment vary with time and with diverse tasks and objectives.

Lateral Thinking

Lateral thinking is a useful mechanism for making decisions. It is a way to explore an issue from all sides by everyone involved. It allows everyone at any given time to be looking in the same direction and focus on finding a way forward (De Bono 1999). De Bono described six directions of thinking by associating them with hats of six different colors:

- white hat: neutral and objective; deals with information, facts, and figures;
- red hat: hunches and feelings; gives the emotional view;
- black hat: careful and cautious; plays the "devil's advocate";
- yellow hat: sunny and positive; represents the optimistic view;
- green hat: creativity and new ideas; offers choices and alternatives;
- blue hat: organization and cool control; makes conclusions and summaries.

Although individuals may feel more at ease wearing specific hats, it is important not to use the hats to label people. It is a positive process that allows each individual to explore one direction at a time while covering all six directions.

Harvesting the Power of Now and Having Fun

Although your mind is very powerful and useful in the pursuit of success and accomplishments, it is imperative to remember that you are not your mind. Do not allow it to take over. It is just a tool—a wonderful tool for you to use and activate. It is up to you to control your mind. This is a feasible and simple task to accomplish. It means creating new habits by initiating the process of positive thinking and visualization followed by passionate repetitive actions. Make sure you are happy and you are having fun. Use appropriate humor. Let your guard down, be passionate, and enjoy everything you do. You can do it now—since now is where everything happens. The present holds the key to your freedom. Make it the primary focus of your life. This does not impair your ability to refer to the past or future for specific practical matters. In fact, it gives you a clearer mind to do so.

"Zero-Based" Governance: A New Model for the Future

A team of effective leaders representing all stakeholders is a prerequisite for successful governance. However, a team that does not see the whole picture is unable to make effective decisions or at best is unable to find the optimum solution. Yet we insist on formulating boards of trustees that do not represent all stakeholders and that are unfamiliar with "zero-based" decision-making and systems thinking. As such, our goal is to ensure that the governing board can see the whole picture, which allows its members to identify all barriers and utilize all the tools available to find optimal solutions.

Before going further, allow me to define the terms introduced above. Systems thinking is a management discipline that concerns understanding a system by examining the linkages and interactions between the components that comprise the entirety of that defined system with the purpose of optimizing it. As for "zero-based" decision-making, it is derived from the concept of "zero-based" budgeting, whereby decisions are made by assessing each area and/or situation based on collective input from diverse assessments in relation to the university's guiding statements (vision, mission, values, etc.). In order to find an optimum design for governance, we must begin by establishing the desired output. In essence, we should redefine our guiding statements so that advancing citizenship and social justice, promoting democracy and human rights, endorsing a learner-centered philosophy, supporting holistic leadership and conflict resolution, offering majors relevant to the needs of local and regional economies, and operating with a business model that is conscious of ethical, social, and environmental issues are at the heart of the vision, mission, and values of every higher education institution. Second, we should include all stakeholders in the governing process. A stakeholder is a person, group, or organization that has an interest in or concern for an institution. Stakeholders can affect or be affected by the institution's actions, goals, and policies. Using this definition and the statements within the redefined guiding statements implies that the list of stakeholders or board members should include students, faculty, administrators, staff, school representatives, business representatives, civic organizations, and government officials, in addition to financial, legal, and environmental experts. All stakeholders should be entitled to see the whole picture and be a part of the planning, implementation, and evaluation stages. Empowering all stakeholders to have a sense of ownership is of utmost importance. Owners have the incentive to optimize systems for maximum value. Although system management may be used at times, the aim is to find an optimum, realistic, and global system design. As for the influence or weight of each of the stakeholders, it should be divided equally between owners, external stakeholders, and internal stakeholders.

"Zero-based" governance—which is based on the concepts of systems thinking, shared governance, holistic leadership, learner-centered education, and redefined guiding statements, as indicated above—is capable of transforming our HEIs into effective, transparent, and ethical institutions. "Hope is life: Change will happen."

References

Adams, B. (2001). *The everything leadership book.* Avon, MA: Adams Media Corporation.

Alsoufi, A., and Jammal, A. (2012). Higher education in Lebanon: National tempus office Lebanon.

Ben-Ruwin, M. (2010). The corporatization of shared governance: The corporate challenge and the Academic Response.

Bergan, S. (2003). Student participation in higher education governance.

Bhandari, R., and El-Amine, A. (2012). *Higher education classification in the Middle East and North Africa: A pilot study.* New York, NY: Institute of International Education.

Blanchard, K., Zigarmi, P., and Zigarmi, D. (2013). *Leadership and the one minute manager: Increasing effectiveness through situational leadership II (updated edition).* New York, NY: William Morrow.

Bruce, A., and Pepitone, J. S. (1999). *Motivating employees.* New York, NY: McGraw Hill.

Bryne, R. (2006). *The secret.* New York, NY: Simon and Schuster.

Burchard, B. (2012). *The change: Activating the 10 human drives that make you feel alive.* New York, NY: Free Press.

Covey, S. (2011). *The 3rd alternative: Solving life's most difficult problems.* New York, NY: Free Press.

De Bono, E. (1999). *Six thinking hats.* (2nd ed). New York, NY: Black Bay Books.

Ghabra, S., and Arnold, M. (2007). "Studying the American Way: An assessment of American-style Higher Education in Arab Countries," Washington Institute for Near East Policy, Policy Focus No 71.

Husni, N. A. (2015). *Leadership and holistic education.* USA: David Publishing Company.

Lasanowski, V. (2010). International branch campuses: Motivations, opportunities, and challenges.

Lau, R. (1996). "Shared governance and Compton Community College District." EDIM 710 Organizational Management and Governance, Pepperdine University Plaza. ED 396806.

Maslow, A. (1954). *Motivation and personality.* New York, NY: Harper.

National Tempus Office Lebanon (2012). Higher education in Lebanon.

Public Schools of North Carolina (2001). *The character education handbook and guide.* Raleigh, NC: Public Schools of North Carolina.

Romani, N. (2009). No.36. Middle East Brief. The Politics of Higher Education in the Middle East: Problems and Prospects.

Schuetz, P. (1999). Shared Governance in community colleges. *Eric Digests.* 4.

Taylor, D. (2003). *The naked leader: The bestselling guide to unlimited success.* New York, NY: Bantam Books.

Tozer, J. (2012). *Leading through leaders. Driving strategy, execution and change.* Philadelphia, PA: Kogan Page.

Trakman, L. (2008). "An outsider's view of governance models: Different models exist for structuring campus governance. Are any of these models right for your institution?" Academe online, http://www.aanp.org/AAUP/pubsres/academe/2008/MJ/Feat/trak.htm?PF=1. (Accessed in June of 2016.)

UN (1999). UN declaration or a culture of peace. Retrieved from http://www.Un-documents.Net/a53r243a.htm. (Accessed in June of 2016.)

UNESCO(month). 23. *The UNESCO 21st century talks.* Paris: UNESCO.

United Nations (UN). (1948) Universal declaration of human rights.

University of Arizona (May 16, 2003). "Implementing shared governance at the University of Arizona." Prepared by Shared Governance Review Committee. http://fp.arizona.edu/senate/Implementing%20shared%20Governance%20%20Best%20Practics.html. (Accessed in June of 2016.)

Wilkens, K. (2011). Higher education reform in the Arab world.

Willoughby, J. (2008). Let a thousand models bloom: Forging alliances with Western Universities and the making of the new higher education system in the Gulf. Working paper series no. 2008-01. Washington, DC: American University, Department of Economics, 2008.

Nabil Husni has 30 years of experience as a teacher, administrator, and educational consultant at colleges and universities in the USA and Lebanon. He has an Ed.D. in Educational Leadership, an M.S. in Applied Mathematics, and a B.S. in Chemical Engineering. He is currently the Principal of Adma International School (LWIS-AIS) and serves as a board member on all the Learner World International Schools (LWIS). He is also a Senior Consultant at School Development Consultants (SDC). His most recent book is entitled *Leadership and Holistic Education.* He is a Peace Maker and a Humanitarian, and the Founder and Servant of the Peace Education Society.

The Impact of Governance in Higher Education Institutions on Scientific Research in the Arab World

Elie Bouri and Mirine Maalouf

The State of Scientific Research in the Arab World

The importance of scientific research in higher education institutions (HEIs) cannot be overstated. Scientific research contributes to the advancement of the knowledge base and understanding of the interaction between two or more variables. In this sense, it can help society overcome a wide range of challenges while producing theoretical and empirical contributions that strengthen student learning and contribute to national development. Scientific research is also one of the drivers of quality in HEIs, as it produces high-quality teachers and enhances the image, reputation, and credibility of the HEIs (Lincoln and Guba 2000). Improving the quality of these features in HEIs plays a central role in the differentiation between research-based and tertiary teaching

E. Bouri (✉) · M. Maalouf
Holy Spirit University of Kaslik (USEK), Jounieh, Lebanon
e-mail: eliebouri@usek.edu.lb; mirinemaalouf@usek.edu.lb

© The Author(s) 2018

G. Azzi (ed.), *Higher Education Governance in the Arab World*,
DOI 10.1007/978-3-319-52060-5_4

HEIs. Generally, high-quality faculty and students are more easily attracted by reputable, research-based HEIs.

In developed countries, HEIs have sufficient capacities to ensure cutting-edge infrastructure and sustained budgets, which contribute to the availability of an adequate research environment. In those countries in particular, research incentives, funding, and technical support have been key elements in enhancing the quality of scientific research in HEIs. Notably, high-quality institutions, doctoral degrees, scientists, and patents are concentrated in Organisation for Economic Co-operation and Development (OECD) countries, mainly in the USA, where science- and technology-based industries and knowledge development have contributed considerably to economic growth. This can be partially explained by the high proportion of expenditure on educational institutions as a percentage of gross domestic product (GDP) (1.6% in OECD countries and 2.6% in the USA).[1]

In developing countries, however, elements that constitute an adequate and stimulating research environment are not systematically available. Generally, insufficient resources and an underperforming infrastructure continue to put constraints on knowledge development. In addition, the lack of sound and sustainable government policy with regard to the higher education system represents a major obstacle to the development of HEIs. In developing countries, the weaknesses in the institutional setting and legal framework, as well as political and economic instabilities, hold back significant progress in the quality of higher education. As compared to developed countries, developing countries on average spend a much smaller proportion of their GDP on educational institutions.

In the Arab world, there is no doubt that HEIs have a key role to play in building the modern state. HEIs have been and continue to be the main source of education for a growing number of students. In parallel, the number of HEIs has expanded significantly to cope with the

---

[1] Source: OECD Education at a Glance 2016 indicators. Tables B2.3 available at: http://www.oecd.org/education/skills-beyond-school/education-at-a-glance-2016-indicators.htm   (accessed January 2017).

increased demand, resulting from the growth in population and the rising awareness of the importance of education. In 1953, the Arab world were home to only 14 universities (public and private), whereas in 2015 we can find more than 600 universities, with at least 250,000 faculty members serving more than 11 million students. Unfortunately, the rise of the educational sector has not been underpinned by national institutional reforms and regulations, or by adequate financial support. According to the latest figures from the World Bank, government expenditure on universities in the Arab world is less than 1.3% of total national income. Compared with the USA and Europe, this represents a major obstacle to the enhancement of the quality of teaching and research in HEIs.

While all Arab countries share a relatively common culture and have few ethnic, religious, and tribal differences, they are at least heterogeneous in terms of population, income, and natural resources. Consequently, in the Arab world, higher education systems and associated research competencies and output exhibit some variety both internally—by institution and sector—and across countries. In some countries, such as Lebanon, Bahrain, Palestine, Qatar, and the United Arab Emirates (UAE), most universities are private, suggesting greater financial and administrative autonomy and more market competitiveness. Conversely, in several other Arab countries, such as Algeria, Iraq, and Morocco, most of the universities are public or affiliated with a higher education council, suggesting a lower level of financial and administrative independence and less market competitiveness. On average, the non-state higher education sector accounts for 36.2% of the total (UNESCO Regional Report 2009). Nevertheless, the success rankings of Arab universities are modest in terms of global rankings; only six Arab universities are among the 400 best universities, according to the QS World University Rankings of 2016. These include King Fahd University of Petroleum and Minerals (189), King Saud University (227), American University of Beirut (AUB) (228), King Abdulaziz University (283), the American University in Cairo (365), and Qatar University (393). According to Altunay and Tonbul (2015), "worldwide ranking success of universities is measured by the quality of the academic staff publications."

A recent trend has emerged in the Persian Gulf in particular regarding the establishment of new foreign HEIs. Following the globalization of higher education services, a number of leading universities in Europe and the USA have established international branch campuses in several regions in the world, such as in China and the Arab Gulf region. In addition, the events of September 11, 2001 have positively impacted the pace of higher education globalization, especially in the Persian Gulf, where several educational academies/cities have been established to host foreign branches of well-known HEIs, such as the Dubai International Academic City (DIAC) and the Education City in Doha. The DIAC hosts, among others, Michigan State University in Dubai, Middlesex University, Saint Petersburg State University of Engineering and Economics, the University of Exeter, the University of Wollongong, the University of Phoenix, and the Rochester Institute of Technology; Education City in Doha hosts Weill Medical College of Cornell University, Georgetown University, Carnegie Mellon University, Virginia Commonwealth University, and Texas A&M University. However, importing higher education from industrialized countries represents an interesting shortcut to establishing a home-made domestic education system, and it also has the advantage of establishing reputable and high-quality education in a timely manner. In some other cases, such as in Lebanon, the number of tertiary universities has increased significantly since 2001 while the overall standards of quality assurance have not been enhanced. This has led to the establishment of many teaching HEIs.

Most Arab countries have established national agencies for the assessment of quality in HEIs. In Jordan, the Higher Education Accreditation Commission was established on March 27, 2005 to supervise quality control in both public and non-public HEIs. It enjoys financial and administrative independence. In the UAE, the Commission for Academic Accreditation (CAA) was established in 2000. In Tunisia, the National Committee of Evaluation (CNE) was founded in 1995. The Saudi Arabia National Commission for Academic Accreditation and Assessment (NCAAA) was established in 2004; it also enjoys financial and administrative independence. In Sudan, the High Commission for Evaluation and Accreditation (HCEA) was initiated in 2003. The

Oman Accreditation Council (OAC) was established in 2001. In Kuwait, the Private University Council for accrediting private universities was initiated in 2000; it is chaired by the Minister of Higher Education and has a membership that comprises eight experts. The National Authority for Quality Assurance and Accreditation of Education (NAQAAE) was established in 2006 in Egypt. In Bahrain, the Academic Accreditation Committee was founded in 2005 and the Association of Quality Assurance and Training was established in 2008. It is worth noting that all of the above-mentioned committees for quality control and quality assurance enjoy a certain level of autonomy; however, each is supervised by its respective national ministry of higher education or council for higher education or is affiliated with the government. Furthermore, most of the above-mentioned quality assurance and accreditation agencies not only function on the national level, but often don't conduct thorough and external peer reviews. Despite the benefits of such agencies for the assessment of quality in HEIs, they most often remain insufficient for the proper development of higher education.

The recent global recognition of the importance of maintaining standards of excellence in research in HEIs has added a new challenge for the Arab educational sector. These standards cover issues such as the knowledge, skills, and attributes required for good teaching and research. Some HEIs in developing countries have taken advantage of this phenomenon and positioned themselves to take advantage of global changes. Such a positioning has obviously relied on extensive resources, which has led many HEIs in developed countries to comply with the accreditation standards of international agencies that have long been established in the USA and Europe. Given that the national quality assurance and accreditations in most Arab countries represent a weak alternative in comparison with international bodies and agencies that utilize external peer reviews and rigorous assessment, several Arab HEIs have tried to obtain international accreditations as a way to differentiate themselves from national average-quality universities. However, research and publications in international refereed journals represent an important requirement for accreditation in a number of faculties. In the process of globalization, scientific research is considered a fundamental condition and criterion for the international positioning of the university. Therefore, academic publishing represents a valuable way to disseminate research papers, scientific articles, and books produced by faculty members in order to maximize impact among practitioners. While several HEIs in the Arab world have progressed in size, their contribution to the scientific literature remains relatively modest. Unlike in industrialized countries, research statistics are not an important policy planning tool for the development of the Arab world. To date, there is no accurate data available on expenditures by governments and HEIs on research skills in the Arab world.

As for the number of scientific publications in the Arab world, the latest figures from Scopus,[2] the well-known and largest abstract database of peer-reviewed literature, including scientific journals, books, and conference proceedings, indicates that the total number of publications in the 16 Arab countries as of September 7, 2016 was 673,977. These cover research output in the fields of science, technology, medicine, social sciences, and arts and humanities. Table 1 presents the data on publications per country. Clearly, the USA is the world leader, with 15,155,226 publications, followed by China and the UK. In the Arab world, Egypt is the leading country in terms of publications, followed by Saudi Arabia and Tunisia. However, the other non-Arab countries from the Middle East and North Africa (MENA) region, Turkey and Israel, have more publications than the entire Arab world (together, Turkey and Israel have 943,883), even though their overall population is lower than that of the Arab world under study. Moreover, after taking into account the size of GDP, all of the Arab world lag behind. The number of publications per million population is shown in Fig. 1.

The leading nation in the Arab world in terms of the number of publications per million population is Qatar (7,218), which is well ahead of Turkey (6,151), but it obviously lags behind Israel (55,433) and the USA (46,758). However, the average number of publications per million population in the Arab world is only 2,011, far below China

---

[2] While other databases for scientific publications—i.e., Web of Science or SCImago JR—exist, we chose to use Scopus, which is the largest database for peer-reviewed literature.

Table 1 Publications in the Arab countries and the rest of the world

Country	Population	GDP (million USD)	Publications	Publications per million population	GDP/Publications
Egypt	93,383,574	330,780	180,975	1,938	1.828
Saudi Arabia	32,157,974	618,274	139,122	4,326	4.444
Tunisia	11,375,220	43,989	67,498	5,934	0.652
Algeria	40,375,954	165,974	49,419	1,224	3.359
Morocco	34,817,065	108,096	47,686	1,370	2.267
UAE	9,266,971	325,135	36,280	3,915	8.962
Jordan	7,747,800	39,795	33,127	4,276	1.201
Lebanon	5,988,153	52,797	25,782	4,306	2.048
Kuwait	4,007,146	106,212	24,237	6,048	4.382
Iraq	37,547,686	148,411	17,462	465	8.499
Qatar	2,291,368	170,860	16,539	7,218	10.331
Oman	4,654,471	51,679	14,536	3,123	3.555
Sudan	41,175,541	93,729	9,766	237	9.597
Bahrain	1,396,829	30,079	5,775	4,134	5.208
Palestine	4,797,239	-	5,212	1,086	-
Mauritania	4,166,463	4,541	561	135	8.094
Arab countries	335,149,454	2,290,351	673,977	2,011	3.398
Turkey	79,622,062	751,186	489,749	6,151	1.534
Israel	8,192,463	306,194	454,134	55,433	0.674
Iran	80,043,146	386,120	374,758	4,682	1.03
USA	324,118,787	18,558,130	15,155,226	46,758	1.225
China	1,382,323,332	11,383,030	4,510,053	3,263	2.524
UK	65,111,143	2,760,960	4,197,993	64,474	0.658
Japan	126,323,715	4,412,600	3,215,919	25,458	1.372
France	64,688,129	2,464,790	2,375,743	36,726	1.037

Notes: Population figures are from http://www.worldometers.info/world-population/population-by-country/ (accessed January 2017); GDP figures are in nominal values from the International Monetary Fund World Economic Outlook April 2016, except for Egypt, which is from the World Bank. Data on scientific publications are from the Scopus database. Notably, the publication data obtained depend on the time of acquisition. Scopus was searched on September 7, 2016

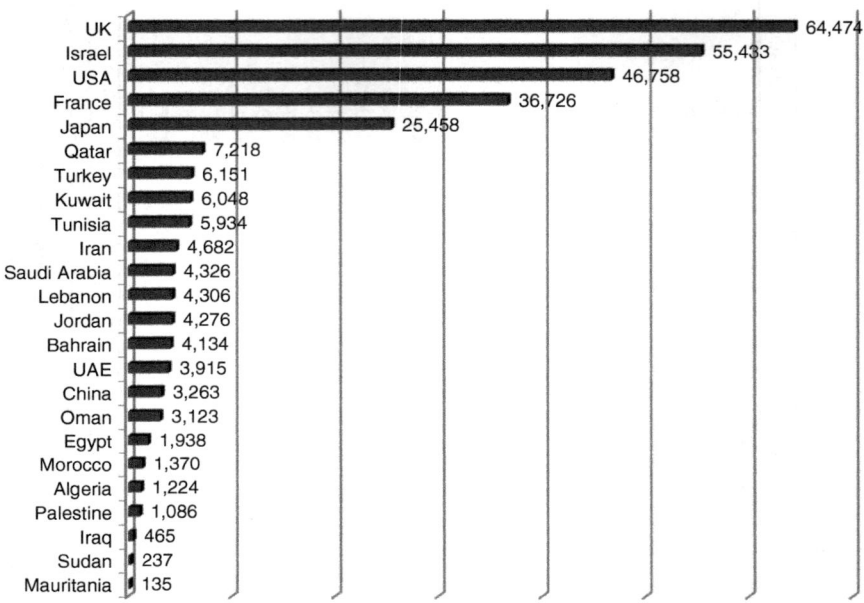

Fig. 1 Publications per million population
Source: See notes to Table 1

(3,263) and Iran (4,682). Regarding the average ratio of GDP to publications, it is behind all the countries under study. Surprisingly, the ratio of GDP to publications in Tunisia (0.652) is considered to be the highest in the region. Another interesting example is Jordan, where the ratio of GDP to publications is bigger than the ratio observed in Turkey, the USA, China, and Japan. These figures suggest major differences across the Arab world in terms of the number of publications they produce.

Prior studies have argued that many factors can lead to a weak result with regard to scientific publications; these include, among others, a weak research background (Meek et al. 2009) and a low share of GDP for higher education (Arab countries 0.2–0.4%; industrialized developed countries 4–6%). The lack of an effective and stable system of higher education funding is one of the major factors that prevent HEIs from conducting and producing serious research. Initiatives for research funding, mainly from governments and government-related entities, remain limited in scope and size. Surprisingly, public funding in the Arab region is more significant and growing at a faster pace than private funding, which remains shy and irrelevant for the development of research. This pattern is the opposite to that found in most OECD countries, where the share of private expenditure grew more than public expenditure (OECD 2003). Another reason for the low rate of publication in the Arab world is the very weak presence of national and international research institutions in the Arab world in comparison to other developing economies. For example, several research institutions receive funds and conduct research in a number of regions outside the Arab world. Among these research institutions, we can mention the Inter-American Institute for Cooperation on Agriculture in Costa Rica, the European Southern Observatory in Chile, the International Rice Research Institute in the Philippines, the International Potato Center in Peru, the International Institute of Tropical Agriculture in Nigeria, the Smithsonian Tropical Research Institute in Panama, and the Institut Franco-Uruguayen de Mathématiques (LIA IFUM) in Uruguay. With the exception of a few European Union initiatives that support the higher education sector in several Arab countries (i.e., the programs Tempus and E-TALEB),[3] there are no regional initiatives to establish centers of excellence in research in order to construct effective systems of scientific research. Instead, most of the research centers operate at the national level and often have inadequate databases and limited international collaborative efforts. Furthermore, their support for research activities is restricted by the limited amount of funds they give to researchers (i.e., the Centre National de la Recherche Scientifique [CNRS] in Lebanon). Some other initiatives that are funded by local governments in rich oil countries in the Persian Gulf are significant but still not widespread in all Arab countries. These include, among others, the Qatar National Research Fund, which supports Qatari and regional

---

[3] The program Tempus supports the modernization of higher education, whereas E-TALEB seeks to develop Professional Standards in Teaching and Learning.

researchers; the Scientific Research Commission in the UAE, which was established in 2008 with the aim of promoting and supporting research activities at public and private HEIs; the Science Council in Oman, which was established in 2005; and the establishment of several Chairs of scientific research in leading universities in Saudi Arabia.

Some academics (see, among others, Osman Mohamed Nour 2011) argue that since Arabic is still the official teaching language of many long-established schools and universities in the Arab world, many researchers have limited English writing skills, preventing them from being published in international refereed journals. Obviously, in HEIs where English is the official teaching language, scholars have more capacity to contribute to the scientific debate. However, this argument is undermined by the fact that in Turkey, where the official teaching language in schools is Turkish and where many university programs are delivered in Turkish, the number of scientific publications is higher than in any Arab country (see Table 1). Research output and research skills development depend on the availability of resources; however, resources are shaped by the development of good governance that leads to a favorable academic environment and culture that actively promote research. For example, several studies highlight the importance of having a central coordinating unit that can mentor and stimulate faculty members so that they will be more engaged in good-quality research activities (Easton et al. 2000). Accordingly, Fielden (2008) argues that a governance structure and regulatory framework are essential to the development of higher education systems. In addition to remuneration, the infrastructure, research facilities, and equipment are all essential in attracting and retaining highly qualified researchers. Preserving these elements represents an ongoing challenge that may constrain research capabilities.

The Importance of Governance in HEIs

In the context of higher education, governance is defined as "the formal and informal exercise of authority under laws, policies and rules that articulate the rights and responsibilities of various actors, including the rules by which they interact, so as to help achieve the institution's academic objectives" (Fried 2006). In other words, the governance structure of HEIs describes how different interested parties (rector, senior management team, supervisory board, heads of units, staff, students, governments, etc.) communicate with each other, what each party is accountable for, and who is accountable to whom.

In fact, there are several conceptual models of governance in HEIs that include, among others, collegial, bureaucratic, political, organized anarchy, professional, service university, enterprise university, and entrepreneurship university.

In recent times, there has been a tremendous change in the nature of governance in general, and more specifically at the university level (Kezar and Eckel, 2004). Globalization, internationalization, and privatization have all done much to shape the current situation, and governance has become increasingly complex and multifaceted and is frequently regarded as a precondition for achieving education, research, and innovation—the main pillars of the Lisbon Strategy. De Boer and File (2009) have identified several problems in the governance of European universities, such as the tendency toward uniformity and egalitarianism in many national higher education systems, too much emphasis on monodisciplinarity and traditional learning and learners, and too little world-class governance.

Most developed countries have agreed to increase public funding for higher education, to grant more autonomy to institutions in managing their financial resources, to establish direct links between results and the amount of public funding allocated, and to encourage the diversification of funding sources as well as the creation of partnerships with research institutes, businesses, and regional authorities. Therefore, the granting of sustainable autonomy to HEIs and the implementation of a quality research culture are considered important interrelated tools that can help to improve the governance of these institutions. Autonomy would require HEIs to be able to establish their own academic and research strategy, including defining research themes, program offerings, curriculum structure, student and faculty member selection, and assessment. This academic autonomy would not be efficient unless correlated with administrative and financial autonomy that would enable HEIs to define their financial strategies, budgeting, and allocation of resources necessary for the good implementation of their academic and research strategies. From this perspective, autonomy is an important challenge for all countries where governments are the primary funding source for HEIs.

In most Arab countries, however, the structure and pattern of higher education is characterized by a centralized bureaucracy, suggesting a high degree of centralization and intervention by governments and/or ministries of education (Osman Mohamed 2011).

In the Arab world, a large number of states thus far have not applied the principles of good governance in several areas, such as the political, social, and economic sectors. Accordingly, it is no surprise that the governance of HEIs is suffering from several shortcomings in these states. Prior studies on Arab HEIs indicate several key governance deficiencies, including weak levels of autonomy and transparency, slow government-run bureaucracies, the absence of national independent accreditation agencies, the centralization of admission procedures, unaccountability of institutional actors to boards of governors or stakeholders other than the state authorities, and political influence in the selection of senior management in HEIs.

However, the governance of Arab public HEIs has shifted from a state-control to a state-supervisory model. While such changes to governance mean more freedom for HEIs, they also entail a shift of accountability from the government to the HEIs themselves. Such a move was motivated by a reduction in the government budget burden entailed by the higher education sector. Accordingly, HEIs must bear more responsibilities in allocating expenditure; signing contracts with other universities, outside agencies, and corporations; and receiving funding. For example, they must set their own tuition fees in an effort to decrease their financial dependence. More importantly, they must control and maintain their standards of excellence in teaching and research. Changes in governance also mean that HEIs have to strengthen their management and improve their image to sustain their competitiveness within a tough market. Globalization also has a role to play in intensifying the competition between national, regional, and international HEIs. In this sense, the reputation and credibility of HEIs can shape students' choice of educational destination. There has been a "reduction of trust" in some Arab universities, suggesting a need for changes in the governance structure, which will have implications for the quality of teaching and research. This suggests the emergence of a higher education market in which highly reputable and research-based HEIs dominate and set the global standards in the higher education market, such as the importance of accreditation. However, international accreditation bodies concur that the most appropriate governance system for higher education is one involving effective leadership inspired by a strong vision and backed by robust strategic planning that responds flexibly to national and regional needs.

There have been efforts in some Arab countries to reinforce the governance of HEIs in two aspects: reinforcing the power of the executive authority, and reinforcing the presence of external members in supervisory bodies. As such, the leadership is divided between the rector and the president of the supervisory board drawn from outside the university. Bringing in more representatives from business and industry has the main objective of reinforcing the bridges between the university and the wider society, and especially between the university and the local business community. It also aims to increase the potential effect of higher education on social development (Eurydice 2000) and to generate fresh and lucrative funding opportunities. An example from Lebanon is the case of the Holy Spirit University of Kaslik (USEK) board of trustees, which was established in 2014 as part of a reform of the governance structure to better address the challenges and prospects faced by the higher education sector in Lebanon and the Arab region.

Scientific research activities and research skills development have also been at the center of contemporary debate about governance in HEIs. In particular, promoting a quality research culture within HEIs represents a main concern. HEIs finally came to realize that this could not happen without the adoption of new strategies and the modernization of the university vision, culture, and governance. This special requirement for research is a very complex and challenging encounter that universities have to face, because while universities are expected to continue to pursue theoretical research, they are now also expected to make breakthroughs in applied fields that promise to generate new practical applications. Moreover, through university–industry partnerships and even start-up companies, HEIs are also increasingly asked to directly stimulate local or state economic development.

In Europe, the European Centre for Strategic Management of Universities has called on member states to nearly double aggregate research and development (R&D) investment and increase the share of industry-sponsored research. At the same time, many universities have developed and implemented a number of systems and procedures to ensure the delivery of high-quality research.

Where do Arab HEIs stand in relation to this perspective on modernized governance (with increased autonomy of institutions) and the research-driven strategy that has conquered the USA and European countries? Are Arab HEIs not affected by Western universities' competitiveness in a global knowledge economy?

The Arab Human Development Reports, sponsored by the United Nations, have acknowledged increasing concern over the health of higher education in the Arab world, which faces major obstacles to achieving the main goals of good governance: education, research, and innovation.

While this alarming situation has not gone unnoticed by Arab governments, educational institutions, and stakeholders, the existing educational system has not been completely reshaped so that it can address the challenges of the twenty-first century. This can be explained by the inappropriate and obsolete governance system of Arab HEIs, deriving from the fact that most universities in the Arab world are governmental institutions, with complete financial and administrative dependency (nomination of presidents of universities, deans, etc.) on governmental authorities.

This enslavement results in governmental interference that prevents HEIs from defining and implementing a unique mission with comprehensive objectives, and creates an unsound environment for the personal and academic development of its members. In addition, the lack of academic and institutional freedom prevents universities' stakeholders from participating in decision-making, voicing their opinions, and promoting scholarly innovation.

The changing relationship between the state and the institutions requires substantial legislative reforms, which in turn necessitate a certain degree of open-mindedness and political liberalism. Regardless of the differences between the administrations in the Arab world, a revolution in the educational sector is not to be expected soon, since all Arab states suffer, in variable degrees, from the same syndrome of political reticence toward granting more autonomy and freedom to their HEIs. This situation has left them helpless and sometimes careless in resolving strategic problems that they may be facing, that is, an increasingly diverse and growing student population, new and changing demands from society, limited or even declining resources, and a high cost of living, not to mention the widening gap between Arab and Western educational institutions.

Despite the fact that budgets allocated by Arab governments for education remain limited and insufficient to meet the growing needs of the educational sector, some governments have reduced education expenditures, forcing universities to increase tuition and fees in order to balance their budgets. This cutting-costs policy, together with the absence of interrelated governance, has affected the integration of a quality research culture among the universities' members.

As a result of this situation, the Arab higher education system is witnessing the development of a poor scientific research environment characterized by lack of focus in terms of research impacts (that tackle actual socioeconomic issues) and strategies, insufficient policies and guidance for faculty members to produce intellectual contributions, low awareness of the importance and impact of good scientific research, insufficient networking opportunities and databases, and, last but not least, inadequate assessment tools for quality assurance in research production.

While no accurate data exist on the number of full-time faculty researchers in Arab universities, all indicators point toward a very low number of full-time faculty researchers.

As already indicated, some wealthy Arab states of the Persian Gulf have chosen to import the solution to their problems by establishing campuses of Western universities and financing research and development centers. Such an attempt to resolve deficiencies in educational quality will remain unfruitful, however, if not complemented by a wide-ranging and coherent strategic plan aimed at replenishing the existing educational structure.

The overall effects of the changed environment are forcing the acknowledgement of serious discrepancies in higher education and the redesign of existing governance systems, aimed at promoting a quality research culture that is capable of tackling its own existing socioeconomic issues and involving all stakeholders in the development of the region.

Summary and Recommendations

It seems that the ongoing governance system in the Arab region is inadequate and inappropriate for the challenges of the twenty-first century, as it is unable to demonstrate full awareness of its operating environment and a coherent strategy in relation to the national and international markets for its programs and services. A rebuilding of the governance system appears to be necessary in order to satisfy Arab personal and societal aspirations, while also measuring up to international education standards to provide a viable developmental outcome.

While most policymakers and practitioners are aware of the need for reform and change, so far insufficient national and regional efforts have been made in this regard. In particular, the importance attached to the role of research has to be reinforced in most Arab HEIs. To deal with the above-mentioned issues and concerns, we suggest the following actions:

- Grant more autonomy for HEIs in both academic and non-academic areas.
- Provide wider access to post-secondary education.
- Tailor a mission to enhance the research culture.
- Enhance the link between current research projects in HEIs and socioeconomic development plans.
- Create innovative policies and incentives to promote and maintain research activities.
- Provide the necessary research infrastructure and facilities.
- Reduce the number of teaching hours for academic faculty.
- Attract highly skilled full-time faculty researchers.
- Ensure a delicate balance between teaching and research activities.
- Set clear guidelines for managing and assessing research.

- Maintain a sustainable level of investment in research as a way to reduce the emigration of qualified researchers.
- Introduce an Arab channel (network) of researchers to exchange research expertise across the Arab world and share scientific research projects.
- Establish a database, mainly primary data, for different fields so that research will be available to Arab researchers.
- Develop centers for excellence in research to complement the role of quality assurance units.

References

Altunay, E., and Tonbul, Y. (2015). Comparison of scientific research projects of education facilities. *Studies in Higher Education*. *40*(6), 972–987.

De Boer, H. F., and File, J. (2009). *Higher education governance reforms across Europe (MODERN project)*. Brussels: ESMU.

Easton, K. L., McComish, J. F., and Greenberg, R. (2000). Avoid common pitfalls in qualitative data collection and transcription. *Qualitative Health Research*, *10*(5), 703–708.

Eurydice (2000). Two Decades of Reform in Higher Education in Europe: 1980 Onwards, Brussels.

Fielden, J. (2008). Global Trends in University Governance, World Bank Education Working Paper Series No. 9.

Fried, J. (2006). Higher education governance in Europe: Autonomy, ownership and accountability – a review of the literature. J. Kohler and J. Huber (eds.), *Higher Education Governance between Democratic Culture*. Council of Europe: Academic Aspirations and Market Forces.

Kezar, A., and Eckel, P.D. (2004). Meeting today's governance challenges. *The Journal of Higher Education*. *75*(4), 371–398.

Lincoln, Y. S., and Guba, E. G. (2000). *Naturalistic Inquiry*. London: Sage.

Meek, V. L., Teichler, U., and Kearney, M. (eds.) (2009). Higher Education Research and Innovation: Changing Dynamics. Report on the UNESCO Forum on Higher Education, Research and Knowledge 2001–2009, International Centre for Higher Education Research Kassel, Kassel.

OECD (2003). *Education at a glance: OECD indicators 2003*. Paris: OECD Publishing.

Osman Mohamed Nour, S. S. (2011). National, regional and global perspectives of higher education and science policies in the Arab region. *Minerva*, 49(4), 387–423.

UNESCO Regional Report (2009). *A decade of higher education in the Arab States: Achievements and challenges*. Beirut, Lebanon: UNESCO Regional Bureau for Education in the Arab States.

Elie Bouri is an Assistant Professor and research coordinator at the Faculty of Business and Commercial Sciences of the Holy Spirit University of Kaslik, where he gives financial markets and financial engineering courses. He conducts research in the fields of corporate governance and financial economics and has published in leading international journals such as *Journal of Management and Governance, International Journal of Business Governance and Ethics, Economic Modelling, International Review of Economics and Finance, International Review of Financial Analysis, Finance Research Letters, Energy Policy, Energy,* and *Energy Economics,* among others.

Mirine Maalouf has a Master's degree in International Administration from Université Paris I- Sorbonne and a graduate degree (Maitrise) in Law from Saint Joseph University, majoring in International Public Law. She is Executive Director of the Arab Society of Faculties of Business, Economic and Political Sciences, lectures on business law and provides legal services to SMEs.

Governance Reform in Higher Education Institutions in the Arab World: An Institutional Initiative

Shafig Al-Haddad and Ayman Yasin

Introduction

The advancement of higher education institutions (HEIs) requires an integrated system of university governance that involves all decision-makers and sources. Thus, governance of universities can vastly improve the value and content of higher education. Saleem (2014) points out that to promote the functions of HEIs (teaching, research, community service), it is essential to develop governance and institutional performance in order to ensure transparency, accountability, and institutional participation of all parties, in accordance with the legislative bodies governing the work (Mar'i 2009). This leads to academic decisions that adhere to the scientific criteria in the councils of HEIs. Furthermore, the weakness in governance that many universities suffer from due to the multiplicity of regulators, authorities, and interveners, as well as personal relationships, leads to a lack of respect for the

S. Al-Haddad (✉) · A. Yasin
Princess Sumaya University for Technology, Amman, Jordan
e-mail: s.haddad@psut.edu.jo; a.yasin@psut.edu.jo

© The Author(s) 2018
G. Azzi (ed.), *Higher Education Governance in the Arab World*,
DOI 10.1007/978-3-319-52060-5_5

recommendations of the governance councils and their decisions (Aal Abbas 2009). Thus, these universities are subject to personal judgments, speed of change, and lack of institutional work and academic criteria (Wilkens 2011).

Accordingly, we find that Arab universities need to recognize the importance of adopting governance standards, the purpose for which they were created, and their role in and contribution to the process of transition to a knowledge-based economy and world of informatics (Al-Shunnaq 2009).

The Arab ministries of higher education and scientific research must adopt a document that lists binding and guiding rules. Universities should be required to adopt the governance responsibilities laid out in this document, which would serve as a road map for universities. The universities could then carry out the reform of the administrative system and adopt more efficient and modern organizational structures (Wilkens 2011; Al-Kayed 2003).

In consequence, the establishment of the governance rules set out to administer the affairs of the universities need "change management" more than anything else. Many of the prerequisites do not need any sort of amendment in legislation, but need to put into action what has already been set out, apply it transparently according to a policy of maximizing achievement, ensure widespread accountability and monitor performance in real reform of HEIs, and develop a prudent management approach. In this system, realism is the most important pillar, and future vision becomes a top priority (Saleem 2014; Constantin et al. 2010; Wilkens 2011; Mar'ie 2009).

Adopting governance systems in universities requires pluralistic, inclusive, and clear governance patterns, in addition to wide participation of stakeholders in strategic decision-making. It also requires the allocation of resources and the existence of supervisory mechanisms among stakeholders to enable them to deal with executive management and guide their behavior. On the other hand, there must exist internal monitoring consisting of the governance council. This council reports on the extent of compliance with regulations and instructions, and the adequacy and efficiency of the internal control system of HEIs (Al-Kayed 2003).

The Beginnings

Saleem (2014) and Al-Shunnaq (2009) state that governance, as a term, began to be widely used by companies in the early 1990s. However, the term was first coined in 1972. At that time, the purpose of governance was set criteria for corporate managers to eliminate the negative practices that harmed business and industry.

The researchers add that the concept of governance was suggested as a possible solution to the crisis universities were facing in 1983, in which departments were established by the executive authority to control students and faculty members. The main task of these departments, as Saleem (2014), Zaharani (2010), and Abdullah (2003) suggest, was to make decisions on behalf of the students and faculty members, who were not able to express their opinions or objections to these decisions. This, in turn, weakened the development of HEIs as academic institutions, leaving them to reformulate the cultural, customary, and scientific trends of society simply because the decision-making was controlled by a handful of people (Wilkens 2011; Aal Abbas 2009; Hénard and Mitterle 2008, inter alia). On the other hand, students and faculty members simply accepted and implemented those decisions without discussing or objecting to them. For example, decisions related to the educational curricula were made with no input from students in the formulation of the curriculum plans and objectives. Moreover, unions and student groups were marginalized, as they were considered target entities. Governance, by contrast, aimed to train students to participate in public life and to strengthen democracy and respect for others (Aal Abbas 2009; Ahrashaw 2007).

Importance of Governance

The importance of adopting governance standards in HEIs in the Arab world lies in its potential to change universities and increase their capacity for excellence and competitiveness (Philippe et al. 2008). Therefore, this chapter aims to access the best resources of governance and develop legislation that guarantees the independence of higher education along with its quality and effectiveness (Barqa'an and Al-Qurashi 2012; Hénard and Mitterle 2008).

This chapter also looks in more depth at the concept of governance and its role in the drafting of legislation governing HEIs in the Arab world. In addition, it addresses ways to activate the governance role by identifying a comprehensive methodology to ensure the independence of universities (Barqa'an and Al-Qurashi 2012). To this end, the chapter highlights some of the successful experiences of governance in higher education and similar sectors in developed countries.

Objectives of Governance

University governance is an integrated system consisting of a set of incorporated and interactive human and material elements that create harmony and balance within the university (Al-Shunnaq 2009).[1] The lack of such a system leads to a major disruption in the operations of the university, and hence its outputs (Saleem 2014: Hénard and Mitterle 2008). The Organisation for Economic Co-operation and Development (OECD) (1999) defines governance as "a set of rules, regulations, procedures, methods and relations that guarantee the proper management of an organization by CEO, board of trustees, stakeholders and other concerned parties to ensure that managers and employees act appropriately and in accordance with the right practices and regulations away from corruption." The United Nations Development Programme (UNDP) defines governance as "practicing the administrative, political and economic authorities to run the society's matters on all levels. Governance is composed of a group of mechanisms, processes and institutions through which interests are met."

---

[1] In this chapter, the word "university" refers mostly to a "higher education institution."

Generally speaking, the application of governance in HEIs has outstanding significance in the contemporary world, since it helps to enhance universities' values and competitiveness, especially with regard to their output and status regionally and globally (Mar'I 2009). The university, then, must work hard to determine its strategic direction by making sound decisions that can serve to maintain the resources and material and moral gains of the university. Thus, the application of governance creates a good atmosphere for collaboration, which seeks to achieve specific goals that target optimal use of the resources of the university (Mar'I 2009).

Governance also strengthens accountability and administers the distribution of tasks and services. Furthermore, it lessens the differences among university staff and increases cases of mergers and interaction among stakeholders. The importance of governance, then, lies in the comprehensive system that, when invested in properly, in accordance with a systematic and scientific approach, makes it possible to adapt to variables in the internal and external environment. Moreover, it reduces differences in point of view and increases integration among stakeholders in order to help achieve competitive advantage in the quality of the material and moral outcomes, and gain an academic reputation at the local, regional, and international levels. Finally, governance helps the university to obtain a global accreditation.

Consequently, governance is not only a comprehensive management of the university, but also represents a broader and deeper concept. It is an integrated system that represents a body of legislation that aims to achieve qualitative processes and outputs in academic and managerial administration. This is all achieved through the selection of appropriate strategies to fulfill the goals of the university. Alternatively, governance is an integrated set of interactive human and material elements that establish harmony and balance within the university. The absence of governance results in major disruption to the operations of the university, and thus to their outputs (Saleem 2014; Hénard and Mitterle 2008).

Major Changes in the Educational System

Governance has become a crucial issue in the field of higher education, which has been undergoing drastic changes since the 1990s (Saleem 2014; Al-Rashdan 2009; Barakat and Milton 2015). These changes include:

- The increasing pressure on HEIs, as both the social demand for higher education and the population are growing. Meanwhile, these institutions are unable to meet this demand for all applicants as a result of the limited capacity of universities.
- The emergence of new programs of education offered by different educational institutions, whether governmental or private. In addition, new forms of education, such as e-learning and distance education, have emerged.
- The weakness of the research infrastructure and the lack of opportunities for scientific research, which takes many forms, including the expansion of programs, especially graduate ones, which lack laboratories and staff. In addition, the culture of scientific research in the public sector and private institutions is becoming weaker. Moreover, links between ongoing research projects at universities and plans for economic and social development, and issues faced by the productive sectors, are declining (Hénard and Mitterle 2008; Ahrashaw 2007).
- The world rankings have increased the pressure to apply governance in universities. The world rankings have three related factors: the concentration of talent, the availability of funding, and governance. Independence allows enterprises to manage their own resources in an appropriate manner and enables them to respond quickly to the changing requirements of the global market (Barqa'an and Al-Qurashi 2012). However, these factors are not enough for a university to attain and retain a position in the global rankings. There is a need for other critical features of governance, such as having inspirational leaders, a strong strategic vision for institutional direction, a philosophy of success and

excellence, and openness to developmental and organizational change (Nufil 1990).

In the face of all these challenges, university governance constitutes a means to bring about change and to meet these challenges, since the methods of managing these enterprises are among the most decisive factors in achieving their objectives (Barqa'an and Al-Qurashi 2012). Therefore, university governance has become a vital component that allows those in charge of these institutions to design and implement guidelines, and to monitor and evaluate the efficiency and effectiveness of universities' performance (Al-Kayed 2003; Mar'I 2009).

Principles of Governance

Saleem (2014), Nassir Al-Deen (2012), Fielden (2008), and the UNDP believe that governance has three principles:

Transparency means clarity about what is happening within the university, with an easy flow of accurate and objective information and ease of use and execution by university staff. This clarity indicates that students can easily disclose thoughts, worries, needs, and problems to their leaders at the university. This, in turn, generates productive dialogue between the leaders of the university and the students. The open meetings provide a challenge to the students' thinking and motivate them to participate in and contribute to the constructive interaction between them and the leaders of the university.

Transparency is also related to the design of the systems, mechanisms, policies, and legislation and to their application. It is one of the important global standards in the classification of countries and even universities, as it is a mechanism to measure the degree of application of governance in the community, which permits individuals to obtain knowledge and information regarding governance so as to enable them to make decisions about whether the institutions are abiding by the laws and regulations (Aal Abbas 2009; Mar'I 2009).

Participation allows governance councils and academic and administrative bodies, students, and the community to participate in policy-making and in the development of business rules in various areas of university life. It also creates opportunities for university students to have a role in the decision-making process. Good governance needs to include all stakeholders in order to support the university leadership and governance councils, and hence become a model for the application of university policies.

Accountability is a commitment that makes parties accountable for all actions and tasks they are asked to do. It enables those who are concerned, inside and outside the university, to monitor work without disrupting it or offending others, and applies the regulations and instructions with full transparency to all workers and students at the university. Accountability is the other face of leadership; without it, dictatorship prevails.

The UNDP includes other principles and characteristics, such as sustainability, legitimacy, equity and equality, and law and order.

Areas of Governance

The areas of governance at a university are varied, but many studies have confirmed that these areas are like the links of a chain, affecting each other and working together to achieve the governance objectives (Saleem 2014; Mausher 2016). These areas include:

The first area: founding commitment and its culture. The governance philosophy is based on the idea of commitment to enrich the culture. It is a lofty and constructive thought, based on long-term and wide educational and moral content (Nufil 1990).

The second area: achieving credibility and increasing confidence in the data and information that are posted about the university, distributing the content of reports to the public, and clarifying what is happening. These can all be reflected positively in the university operations and outputs.

The third area: improving transparency and achieving clarity. This represents a tool of governance that sheds light on the different aspects of the university. Thus, it reduces uncertainty, lack of clarity, and confusion. The more powerful the governance is, the more effective it is, since it improves the degree of transparency and clarity.

The fourth area: attracting local and international investment. Governance is not an end, but a means to achieve multiple objectives related to the university and its strategy.

The fifth area: achieving justice and applying the principle of "equality," as governance creates equal opportunities for all. Applying this principle increases the sense of justice, fairness, and thus safety. These all contribute to eliminating deficits, greed, and corruption (Barqa'an and Al-Qurashi 2012).

The sixth area: administering the university well. Governance administers the university work efficiently and effectively, especially the work that relates to planning, regulation, guidance, and follow-up. This improves the administrative abilities of the university by identifying specific activity goals, determining executive programs, and mobilizing resources and capabilities. In so doing, the achievement of the university's goals is ensured.

The seventh area: increasing efficiency and attention. Governance plays a very important role in improving the efficiency of the university, and makes for a promising present and future through several means, including improving quality, and gaining competitive advantages for university graduates (Hénard and Mitterle 2008; Al-Kayed 2003).

Special Committees

In addition to the various councils, the university monitors its work through several committees. The most important is the finance committee, which has to submit its reports to the general council regarding the financial activities and actions that have taken place at the university. Second, the audit committee, which consists of two non-executive directors and three executive members, reviews the university's systems, monitors its internal by-laws, undertakes risk management, and reviews the effectiveness of the financial system at the university. It also submits a report on the audit of the accounts of the university, and recommends the appointment of an external reference (Hénard and Mitterle 2008; Mutair 2005).

Finally, through the audit committee, the internal audit report has to be submitted to the general council and the executive director of the university. The report reviews the efficiency of risk management, internal control, and governance arrangements at the university. The internal auditors at the university provide reasonable assurance about these matters.

Governance Models

There are four clear models of governance: *the academic model, the corporation model, the stakeholder model,* and *the trustees model* (Saleem 2014).

Governance models led by academics are considered to adhere most closely to tradition. These models adopt the assumption that universities should be subject to the governance of the academic staff. There are several ways to implement such an approach, including giving the power of decision-making to an academic board or to the board of trustees (Aal Abbas 2009). Otherwise, the academic staff have effective representation in the councils of governance, or a prominent academician is appointed as a president or an official in the organization. In academic governance, the academic staff have broader representation and input, and more power in determining the mission of the university.

Compared to governance in the stakeholder model, governance in the trustees model grants the administration to the authority of a board of trustees, which includes members who are not active in the university. Moreover, they do not represent all stakeholders. The board of trustees usually has responsibilities including those related to the duty of the Secretariat and others relating to the protection of guardianship as well as the announcement of any factors that constitute a conflict of interest and guardianship (Al-Farra 2013). The stakeholder model assigns governance to a wide range of stakeholders, including students, faculty members, staff, alumni, supporting companies, the government, and the local community.

Standards and Stages of the Application of Governance in Universities

Many studies that have discussed university governance have confirmed that there are standards that reflect and illustrate the values that should prevail and affect university governance (see Saleem 2014; Al-Shunnaq 2009). These are:

- The existence of laws, regulations, and instructions illustrating best practices for the authority of governance councils in the university (board of trustees, the University Council, the Council of Deans, faculty councils, department councils) as well as the administrative leadership.
- The participation of employees and the local community of non-members of governance boards in decision-making, and in directing the course of action at the university (Aal Abbas 2009).
- The extent to which governance councils and staff at the university assume their responsibilities.
- The presence of main committees supervised by the governance boards, which address matters that need further research and detailed study.
- The degree of disclosure of the salaries, rewards, and achievements that members of the governance boards and staff have attained.
- The degree to which local, Arab, and regional quality assurance standards are applied (Hénard and Mitterle 2008).

The standards mentioned above are basic pillars of five phases/stages proposed for the application of governance in universities:

Phase I: spreading the culture of governance and organizing campaigns to sway public opinion in the university's favor. This is the most important stage, because it clarifies the different aspects of governance, which include its landmarks, dimensions, concepts, curricula, tools, and missions. At this stage, a clear distinction is made between governance as a culture, attitude, and commitment, and governance as the basis for honest interaction.

Phase II: building governance. At this stage, a strong infrastructure capable of absorbing governance movement and incorporating current and future variables is set up. It is an accumulated, complex, and extended structure consisting of a primary superstructure of governance and including governance boards as well as supervisory committees that apply governance at the university level. There is also a primary infrastructure of governance that includes the ethical and moral foundations.

Phase III: developing a procedural plan for governance. At this stage, goals, tasks, and duties are determined.

Phase IV: implementing and applying governance. Governance, here, is implemented precisely with the development and review of each step. In this phase, the willingness of all parties to implement governance is properly tested and measured for the first time (Hénard and Mitterle 2008).

Phase V: following up and developing governance. In this stage, it is important to ensure the good implementation of all previous stages. Oversight and follow-up are considered the means and main administration tools used by the university to ensure proper implementation of governance. It is an integrated censorship that has preventive, innovative, and remedial functions.

The Role of Students in Governance-Based Universities

Governance in universities is distinct from other management systems because it puts the student first and he/she is the axis of all its operations. If governance is based on the participation of students in the policies, decisions, and mechanisms that will allow the university to achieve its objectives of providing excellent educational service and monitoring and evaluating it, then how can we translate this into practical application, and by a procedural method that can measure the level of students' participation in the administration of the university (Saleem 2014)?

At the outset, this requires the system to determine the roles and responsibilities of each party and to hold all parties accountable.

Individuals' and parties' performance is evaluated publicly and transparently according to the nature of the role and the size of their mandated responsibilities (Mar'I 2009). This indicates that there should be a reformation of the relationship between the university administration and students. Within this frame, the missions and roles of students can include participating in the development of university policy and management decisions with respect to academic and non-academic matters that affect them directly. Students' practice of this role is one of the important elements in the development of their personalities, and it trains them to think deeply and understand problems and contribute to a state of coordination between students, faculty members, and administrative staff. This, in turn, increases their affiliation and loyalty to the university, fosters the ability to deal with societal problems, and instills in them a sense of belonging and loyalty to the local community.

The students have many positive tasks within the framework of the application of governance in the university. First, they can participate in the development of plans for student activities outside the classroom. The places where these activities are conducted should enjoy the broadest measure of freedom (Al-Nashif 2001). When this happens, the students feel a real sense of responsibility, that they play an important role in the university, and that their views have a significant impact on the development of the university and on activating its internal and external roles (Ahrashaw 2007).

Second, the students can participate in the administration of the university when decisions are taken regarding the development of educational programs, or about the introduction of new educational programs that meet their needs and the needs of the local community (Barqa'an and Al-Qurashi 2012; Aal Abbas 2009). This has great impact, since it makes them feel a sense of obligation toward that role. In addition, their participation in the assessment of the university administration and the evaluation of teachers and educational programs will also foster a sense of responsibility. This will be very beneficial in developing the whole educational process. Eventually, it will lead to higher-quality outputs.

Moreover, under the application of governance, students should be given ample opportunity to contribute to the campus atmosphere by forming whatever entities they choose, rather than participating only in the ones imposed on them. Furthermore, they should have the right to form student unions in a democratic way, which will provide practical experience in political participation and facilitate the development of leadership skills.

These responsibilities and other modes of participation must be exercised with the greatest amount of freedom, so that their responsibilities become clear. Accordingly, their performance can be evaluated and they can be held accountable for their actions and decisions. This will only be achieved if there is a genuine belief within the university community that young people, with their initiatives and their creativity, are capable of contributing to the development of the educational process as well as that of the university and the whole community (Mar'I 2009; Hénard and Mitterle 2008; Al-Nashif 2001).

The Negative Effects of the Non-Application of Governance in Universities

University governance is one of the most important means for improving the quality of leadership and management, of performance, and of processes and outputs (Hénard and Mitterle 2008). Higher education and its institutions represent a suitable ground for the application of rules and principles. The best example is the success of the application of governance in universities in the UK, since those universities have clearly and effectively attained advanced levels in the world rankings of universities.

Therefore, the application of governance in universities should include all of the components, since the university forms a ground for an integrated system. It consists of a set of overlapping, interlocking, and interactive elements that seek to achieve specific goals. However, in the case of non-application of university governance, this will negatively affect the rules and principles of governance and hence its operations, outputs, leadership, management, and internal and external environments. Saleem (2014) maintains that these effects include, but are not limited to:

Transparency: The lack of transparency will lead to:

- the university's inability to obtain an international ranking, as transparency is one of the standards in the world rankings of universities;
- the inability to enforce, or weakness in enforcing, laws, regulations, and instructions objectively on all workers and students at the university;
- the inability of individuals to access knowledge and information related to governance, which would enable them to make accurate and objective decisions. This leads to difficulties for workers at universities in using and applying the rules and regulations;
- the absence of an exchange of ideas between the leaders and departments of the university themselves, and between members of the university, or between them and the students, and a lack of communication between all the parties in all university operations;
- the inability to define roles and tasks for all those in charge of the educational process and administrative tasks;
- the inability to objectively and transparently choose leaders, university administrators, and members of the academic and administrative staff.

Accountability: The absence of accountability will lead to:

- the inability to apply the regulations and by-laws transparently and objectively to all university personnel and students (Hénard and Mitterle 2008);
- the lack of accurate reports by audit and censorship committees at the university to see how effective and efficient the financial systems at the university are, as well as the lack of accurate reporting on the auditing of the university's accounts (Mutair 2005);
- the lack of control among stakeholders that enables them to deal with the executive management and direct their behavior through repeated electoral mechanisms;
- the university's inability to disclose its financial statements, accompanied by separate reports by the auditors to the community and members of the university because of the lack of an

integrated system of external and internal evaluations and the lack of a follow-up system (Mutair 2005).

Participation: The absence of participation will lead to:

- the leadership and management of the university, academic and administrative staff, the students, and the community in general not taking part in drawing up the university's policies, regulations, instructions, and by-laws (Hénard and Mitterle 2008);
- students not being allowed to make decisions or participate in preparations for decision-making (Aal Abbas 2009);
- stakeholders not participating in making strategic decisions about the university;
- faculty members and administrative staff and students refraining from participating in all the activities of the university and not assuming societal responsibility.

Result of the Non-Application of Governance in Universities

Based on what has been presented above, when contemplating the three rules of governance as a system, we find that there are some interactions that occur between them. The absence or weakness of these rules will lead to an imbalance in the interaction, and this, in turn, will lead to (taken from Saleem 2014):

1. an increase in corruption, since the governance rules and their interaction are essential to fight corruption and overcome its consequences. In addition, academic corruption, which is the greatest threat to the reform projects in universities, will spread. The most common form of such corruption is misusing academic authority and diverting it for one's personal interests (Al-Farra 2013);
2. a decrease in investments, especially in private universities, and a decrease in partnerships with economic enterprises. The reason is

that investors are unwilling to invest in a university that suffers from corruption;

3. a loss of credibility with regard to the university's operations and outputs, the spread of non-accountability, and the lack of practical, professional, or moral commitment;

4. a total loss of rights and commitments and an increase in alienation and separation from reality. These all lead to fraud, forgery, and the use of any illegal means to distort truth. The result is the creation of a false state that does not reflect what is going on in the university;

5. an increase in non-belonging and non-commitment. The workers no longer abide by the rules and regulations, which can lead to bribery, nepotism, and reversal of standards;

6. the spread of violence and riots due to the absence of accountability, participation, and transparency;

7. an inability to democratically form governance councils. Even when they exist, they are unable to perform their tasks fully and assume their responsibilities;

8. isolation from society and neglect of its needs. Universities no longer bear their societal responsibility (Al-Yusuf 2000);

9. lack of a clear vision or policy to develop the capacity of those who work at the university, as well as a failure to develop their skills and performance and to change their thinking, starting with students and ending with the university president. This will adversely affect the research and learning processes (Mar'I 2009).

Problems Encountered by Arab Higher Education

The Arab world suffers from a set of problems that adversely affect higher education. These are summarized below (Al-Rashdan 2009).

1. Most universities in the Arab world do not have a philosophy on which they can build a realistic educational policy, which in turn leads to the lack of a clear strategy for higher education (Nufil 1990).

2. HEIs suffer from a participation crisis in management. Government employees run these universities and they generally seek to serve their institutions. Therefore, the scientific and educational work at the universities is negatively affected (Abdullah 2003).
3. Arab universities do not maintain control of their surroundings because the residents of the neighboring houses and the government sometimes control that surrounding environment.
4. Most universities have weak relations with other universities, and the lack of cooperation between them prevents discussion of mutual problems. As a result, most Arab universities tend to collaborate with non-Arab universities to resolve their problems.
5. Most Arab HEIs adopt traditional forms of education, which rely on rote memorization of material, without giving the students any chance to be innovative or to apply their scientific knowledge in practice (Barqa'an and Al-Qurashi 2012). Consequently, students are not urged to adopt an analytical approach to the problems they face in society, which creates a fear of expressing their opinions (Al-Yusuf 2000).
6. Most university programs are poorly integrated because the curricula do not incorporate any kind of unified standards.
7. Universities lack technical, legal, and institutional frameworks, and therefore resort to ad hoc solutions.
8. The pre-university stage and university education are poorly linked. The university curriculum does not follow on from what the students have already learned in high school, so most of the knowledge is new to students and is different from what they have already learned.
9. Finally, most HEIs rely on traditional methods in management. This, in turn, means that the concept of comprehensive quality management, which is far more effective than any of the traditional methods, is ignored (Barqa'an and Al-Qurashi 2012).

Conclusion

Higher education has a major role to play in building modern Arab countries and preparing qualified employees and workers in different fields. Higher education deepens values of national allegiance and fidelity, while broadening individuals' horizons and instilling in them a sense of responsibility to solve the problems that their societies face (Boumalham 1999). Despite what they have accomplished, HEIs face numerous obstacles that impede their ability to catch up with the modern world's demands. The solution to these problems lies in adopting the concept of governance: an integrated system that consists of interactive human and material elements that create harmony and balance at work (Hénard and Mitterle 2008). The absence of governance, then, creates terrible dysfunction in the processes and outputs. Accordingly, this chapter offers the following recommendations:

1. Increase the number of university governance members in the universities generally and on the boards of trustees in particular so that they are proportionate to the size of the university.
2. Involve local community members who have competences related to the specializations offered at the universities.
3. Activate the governance councils in the universities so that they assume their societal and national responsibilities in all aspects (Boumalham 1999).
4. Work hard to develop regulations that stress the real independence of universities in their financial and administrative functions (Barqa'an and Al-Qurashi 2012; Mutair 2005).
5. Expand the culture of governance, including the principles of accountability, transparency, and participation, which will be positively reflected in the performance and efficiency of universities. This will enable universities to attain international rankings in various fields (Saleem 2014).
6. Review the by-laws related to each university's governance concepts and implementation. Such a review should be held annually so as to amend the inactive articles and add new laws that cope with the current status of the university and the workers and students in it. The laws also must take into consideration international trends in university governance (Hénard and Mitterle 2008; Mutair 2005).
7. Prepare awareness programs about governance and its principles and implementations for the students, the faculty members, and the administrative staff, especially the new ones, by holding seminars, lectures, and workshops on the topic.

8. Democratize education, create greater university autonomy, and link higher education with sustainable development, all of which will contribute to proper reform of higher education (Wilkens 2011).

References

Aal Abbas, Mohammad (2009). Hawkamat Al-jaami'aat: Diraasah Tahleeliya' [Governance of universities: An analytical study]. A paper presented at the *Symposium of Governance of Corporates and the Current Practices and Future Horizons*. Abha King Khaled University, KSA.

Abdullah, Mohammed (2003).Azmat al-ta'lim al-'ali fi al-watan al-'arabi wal-tahaddiyat al-mu'asira – waqi' wa-bada'il' [Higher education crisis in the Arab nation and contemporary challenges—reality and alternatives]. *Shu'un Arabiya* (113), 129.

Aghion, Philippe, Dewatripont, Mathias, Hoxby, Caroline M., and Mas-Colell, Andreu (2008). The information network on education in Europe (Eurydice). In Belgium European Commission, *Higher education governance in Europe*. Belgium: European Commission, Eurydice.

Ahrashaw, Al-Ghali (2007). 'Al-siyasa al-ta'limiya wa-khutat al-tanmiya al-'arabiya – hasila wa afaq' [Educational policy and Arab development plans—results and prospects]. *Shu'un Arabiya*, 107, 141.

Al-Farra, majid (2013). Al-hawkama fi mu'assasat Al-Ta'leem Al'Ali fi filisteen-Hala Dirasiya li Kulliyat Al'Ulum Al-iqtisadiya wa al-idiariya fi Ghaza' [Governance in higher education institutions in Palestine—A case study of the administration and economics faculties in Gaza]. In Zaytounah University, *The third arab international conference for quality of higher education*. Jordan: Al-Zaytoonah University.

Al-Kayed, Zuhair (2003). *Al-hakmaniya: qadaya wa tatbiqat' [Governance: Issues and applications]*. Egypt: Al-Munathama Al-Arabiya li-Altanmiya Al-Idariya.

Al-Nashif, Taysir (2001). *Al-sulta wal-hurriya al-fikriya wal-mujtama [Power, intellectual freedom, and society]*. Beirut: The Arab Institution for Studies and Publishing, 100.

Al-Rashdan, Abdul-Fattah (2009). Al-ta'leem Al-'ali fi Al'alam Al'arabi: aamaal wa Tahadiyat [Higher education in the Arab world: Hopes and challenges]. Department of Political Science, Mu'tah University, *Jordan*, pp. 77–90.

Al-Shunnaq, Radi (2009). Mafhoom Al-Haakimiya wa darajat mumarasatiha fo Al-Jaami'aat Al-Urduniya Al-khassa' [The concept of governance and the degree of practicing it in the Jordanian private universities]. Unpublished PhD, Educational Administration Department, The University of Jordan: Jordan.

Al-Yusuf, Ahmad (2000). 'ilaaqat al-tarbiya bil-mujtama' wa-tahdid malamihha al-naw'iya' [Education's relationship with society and determining its quantitative features]. *Alim al-Fikr*, 1, 18–23.

Al-Zahrani, Khadija (2010). Waqi' tatbeeq al-hawkamah Al-rashida fi Al-Jaami'aat Al-Ahliya Al-Saudiya wa 'alaqatiha bi-lrida Al-Wathifi li-A'daa' hay'at Al-Tadrees feeha' [The current status of applying governance in Saudi private universities and its relation with the faculty members' satisfaction]. Unpublished PhD, Educational and Planning Department. Umm Al-Qura University: Makka.

Barakat, Sultan, and Milton, Sansom (2015). *Houses of wisdom matter: The responsibility to protect and rebuild higher education in the Arab world*. Washington, D.C., Foreign Policy at Brookings, pp. 1–11.

Barqa'an, Ahmad, and Al-Qurashi, Abdallah (2012). Hawkamat Al-jaami'aat wa dawriha fi muwaajahat al-Tahadiyat' [Governance of universities and its role in facing the challenges]. A paper presented at the *International Conference of Globalization of Administration in the Globalization Era*. Al-Jinan University, Lebanon.

Boumalham, Ahmad (1999). Azmat al-ta'lim al-'ali–wajhat nazar tatajawiz hadud al-aqtar' [Higher Education Crises—A Point of View Going Beyond National Borders], Beirut, *Majallat al-fikr al-'arabi*, no. 98.

Constantin, brătianu, Zeno, Reinhardt, and Oana, Almăşan (2010). Practice models and public policies in the management and governance of higher education. *Transylvanian Review of Administrative Sciences*, vol. 26, pp. 39–50.

Development. Council. Meeting, & Development. Council. (1999). *Meeting of the OECD Council at Ministerial Level: 26–27 May 1999: A Synthesis. OECD.*

Fielden, John (2008). *Global trends in university governance*. Sweden, Education Working.

Hénard, Fabrice, and Mitterle, Alexander (2008). *Governance and quality in higher education*. Paper Series 9.USA: The World Bank.

Mar'I, Mohammed (2009). Al-hawkama Al-Akadimiya bayna Al-Takhteet Al-istratiji wa qiyas Al'Adaa' Al-mu'assasi' [Academic governance and strategic planning to measure institutional performance]. A paper presented to the Third Scientific Conference of Academic Governance. School of Business Administration and Educational Sciences in Ruh Al-Qudus University: Lebanon.

Muasher, Marwan (2016). 'Tahseen Al-Haakimiya fi Al-Alam Al-arabi' [Improving governance in the arab world]. *The Second Arab Awakening and the Battle for Pluralism.*

Mutair, Ra'fat (2005). 'Aaliyat tad'eem dawr al-muraaja'a al-hukumiya fi hawkamat al-sharikaat' [Mechanisms of supporting the role of Governmental review in corporate governance]. *majalat Al-Jami'a Al-islamiya,* 13(1), pp. 121–137.

Nassir, Al-Deen, Ya'qub (2012). '*Waqi' Tatbiq Al-Hakimiya fo Jami'at Al-sharq Al-Awsat' [The current state of applying governance in the Middle East University].* Amman: Manshuraat Al-sharq Al-Awsat.

Nufil, Mohamed Nabil (1990). "ta'ammulat fi falsafat al-ta'lim al-jami'i al-'arabi' [Reflections on Arab university education philosophy]' *Majallat al-Tarbiya al-Jadida,* 151, 17.

Saleem, Maher (2014). 'Intishar thaqafat al-hakimiya yusa'id 'ala ta'zeez ada' al-jaami'aat' [The Spread of Governance Culture Helps to Promote the Performance of Universities]. *Diraasaat,* The University of Jordan.

Wilkens, Katherine (2011). *Higher education reform in the Arab world.* Washington, D.C., Saban center at Brookings, pp. 1–13.

Shafig Al-Haddad has been Professor of Marketing and the Dean of King Talal Faculty of Business & Technology at Princess Sumaya University for Technology (PSUT) in Amman, Jordan, since 2015. Previously he worked at Applied Science University, Jordan (1991–2014); was Acting President of the Applied Science University (2012–2013); Vice President of Applied Science University (2011–2014); Dean of Scientific Research and Graduate Studies at Applied Science University (2010–2014). Finally, he served as a member of the editorial board of the *Business Administration Journal,* University of Jordan (2012–2016). He was also the Chairman of the editorial board of the *Jordan Journal of Applied Science* (2010–2014).

Ayman Yasin is currently the head of the Coordination Unit for Service Courses at Princess Sumaya University for Technology in Jordan. He studied linguistics at Purdue University in Indiana, USA (2008–2012). He is interested in social sciences in general and in linguistics in particular. He has published papers on syntax, phonology, translation, and cinema. He has also taught Master's courses in linguistics and translation at the University of Jordan. He is an IELTS examiner at the British Council and he serves as a reviewer for three journals.

The Role of Governments in Shaping Governance of Higher Education Institutions in the Arab World

Antoine Habchi

Introduction

Higher education arose as a response to society's needs in the domain of production; professional teaching satisfied these needs and continued to evolve over decades, reflecting the increasing needs and the technical evolution of the market. The more complex and diversified the production became, the more the higher education services reflected this complexity and diversification. However, people's needs were not related solely to the market or to technological innovation; the human anxiety was related to the understanding of individuals, societies, and different dimensions of human sciences. The search for the truth was and remains the ultimate objective.

The administration of higher education institutions (HEIs), which are influenced by culture and by government policies, requires a governance system. The independent states that arose in the Arab world after the

A. Habchi (✉)
Holy Spirit University of Kaslik (USEK), Jounieh, Lebanon
e-mail: antoinehabchi@usek.edu.lb

© The Author(s) 2018
G. Azzi (ed.), *Higher Education Governance in the Arab World*,
DOI 10.1007/978-3-319-52060-5_6

Second World War are characterized by a very specific pattern of interaction between governments and HEIs. Indeed, the role of government in higher education governance reflects the traditional evolution of the relationship between governments and HEIs; it is linked to the nature of political regimes in the Arab world and determines the model of higher education governance. This chapter describes the role of government in the higher education system in the Arab world through, first, a description of the historical evolution of higher education governance generally, and in the Arab world in particular; second, a definition of the role of government and its implications in the Arab world; and third, an analysis of the nature of the interaction between governance and political regimes.

Historical Evolution of Higher Education Governance

The domain of higher education initially was controlled entirely by religious institutions. The Catholic Church began to offer a Master's degree in Italy in the twelfth century. These degree holders, who specialized in theology, law, or medicine, were then allowed to teach anywhere. In order to pursue the degree, one needed to have completed a Bachelor's degree offering mastery of Latin grammar, persuasive thinking and logic, music studies, mathematical knowledge (arithmetic and geometry), and astronomy.

Those who had obtained the Master's degree then taught courses in these subjects at universities (Perkins 1984). The first revolution in university teaching occurred with Thomas Aquinas through the use of Plato's dialogues, introducing his dialectical method of questioning all presumptions, even religious ones. It was the beginning of the separation of the university and the Church, based on the idea that the mission of a university is to search for the truth independently of any religious bonds or beliefs, despite the fact that universities were financed by the Church or through the Church by private investors. On October 1517, Martin Luther presented a protest of ninety-five questions to the pope where he discussed various issues. This initiative gave birth to public education (Perkins 1984).

For Martin Luther, it was critical to ameliorate public molarity through educating children in government controlled institutions not in schools controlled by the Catholic church as was the case at that time (Helmreich 1959).

Several political leaders sponsored schools in their states among which was Prince Frederick III, the Elector of Saxony-Germany, who was one of the early supporters of Martin Luther and his reformation act. This public education system was expanded during the eighteenth century under Frederic William I and later Frederic the Great. Education was obligatory for all children, and government controlled the private teaching of the Church in order to promote religious tolerance among citizens, considering that the only common loyalty should be to the state or nation (Helmreich 1959).

Public education, controlled and funded by governments, flourished in the nineteenth century in various European countries (such as France and England), which sought the creation of a popular education that promoted common values and attitudes and would result in the consolidation of national unity (Glenn 1988) and recognition of the right to be different in multicultural societies, which was necessary to create harmony between people with different cultural backgrounds (Hyman and Wright 1979).

Historical Evolution of Higher Education

The number of universities increased after the twelfth century. Sixteen universities in the thirteenth century became 38 in the fourteenth century, and 72 in the fifteenth century. The ownership of these universities shifted during the nineteenth century from religious institutions to the state, mainly with the development of the native state concept (Bowman 1962). It was not until after 1917 that government control was established over higher education in the Soviet Union, giving the Communist Party an exclusive directive role in all educational institutions, a development that occurred again, largely in the same direction, after the collapse of the Soviet Union and the rise of the Russian Federation (Hyneman 1995, 1997). In the Arab world, higher education was primarily related to multiconfessional orders. Funded by endowments, the most well-known and prestigious among them was Al-Azhar in Egypt, founded around 970. The main curriculum of these universities was the Islamic religion, although nonreligious sciences were taught in some universities.

The Ottoman Empire sent scholars to Europe to study and gain experience so they could implement European modernism back home; in the nineteenth century, the Egyptian Mohammad Ali established several HEIs in Egypt that copied the European model. During the same period and mainly from the end of the seventeenth century, educational institutions were founded by European missionaries and American Protestants in the Middle East and North Africa (MENA) region.

During the modern period, the rise of HEIs in the Arab world has evolved only in the twentieth century. Only 14 universities existed in the region before 1953: Al-Azhar (founded in 1910), Egyptian University (1908), American University of Cairo (1919), University of Farouk the First (1938), and Ain Shams University (1950) in Egypt; American University of Beirut (AUB) (1866), Saint Joseph University (1897), and Lebanese University (1951) in Lebanon; Al Mustansiryah (1984) in Iraq; the Syrian University (1923) in Syria; University of Algiers (1909) in Algeria; Al QaraWiyeen University (1859) in Morocco; Al Zaytoniah University (1734) in Tunisia; and the University of Khartoum (1902) in Sudan. The boom in establishing HEIs, mainly by the private sector in the Arab world, only occurred at the end of the twentieth century and the beginning of the twenty-first. Today, there are about 600 universities in the Arab world, among which almost 250 are private institutions. This development has been supported partly by governments and partly by private investments. The earliest universities in the Arab world were owned by confessional orders, either Islamic or Christian. In the wake of decolonization and the foundation of independent countries in the Arab world, governments took on a greater role in higher education at the end of the last century and the beginning of the current one. Private investments and the number of international universities increased, and higher education played an increasing role in shaping society. The complexity of HEIs' curricula and the rising competitiveness of the market led to new ideas about the way these institutions were governed and the state's role in the governance of HEIs.

History of Higher Education Governance

The term "governance" refers to the capacity of the public and private sectors to cooperate in order to ensure the well-being of society as a whole and to create social opportunities. Governance in higher education is about determining the power and authority that is given to different stakeholders interacting together to take decisions within universities. These decisions and struggles over power involve the governance and the administrative structure of HEIs. How responsibility is spread and what the tools of accountability are seem to be the main governance questions in higher education (Corcoran 2004). These elements are those of internal governance, which involves the institutional components of HEIs, their authority relations, and the procedures of administrative processes; elements related to national law, rules, and quality of teaching, which comprise external governance, also affect the governance of HEIs. The interaction of internal and external governance forms what is called higher education governance (Boer and File 2009).

Internal governance has been the subject of a large volume of literature (Rowlands 2013), but an exploration of external governance is needed in order to gain a deep understanding of internal governance, since the two are related. This interrelationship has gained more significance in the context of globalization and the open market, which have given an essential role to government and market forces (Neave 2003).

Thereby, we can understand the evolution of higher education governance as a response to social changes affecting, in theory and in practice, the role of governments in society and, by extension, in higher education governance.

Between the twelfth and the sixteenth centuries, major changes occurred in European societies, which created the need for technical skills and also for professional training, resulting in professional teaching. The technical nature of HEIs addressed the amplified needs resulting from urbanization, socioeconomic development, the expansion of the middle class, and mercantilism in international commerce (Cobban 1992). Universities were a platform for cooperation and partnership between students and their teachers, providing mutual financial benefit (Haskins 1957). Political authority (government) did not intervene, allowing educational institutions full autonomy to ensure the well-being of their human constituencies (Schechter 2006). Between the sixteenth and the nineteenth centuries, Europe witnessed the proliferation of nationalism and the independence of nation states. Indeed, each nation state was defined by clear and identifiable borders, a population related to each other through a feeling of attachment to the same nation, and a monarchy representing and governing the nation. This political evolution led to a change in the concept and at the same time the function of the university. Its new task was not only to teach, but also to serve the community (Scott 2006). The ultimate objective of the university became service to the political regime. A new interactive relationship arose between universities and political authorities. The former were transformed into sociopolitical tools that served the government and defended its ideology; the latter (the government) perceived universities as institutions of the state that should support and protect its actions (Readings 1996). During this phase, universities lost their academic autonomy, serving instead the interests of the nationalist culture.

The Humboldtian approach, which influenced the higher education system throughout Europe and the rest of the world, was developed during the first decade of the nineteenth century. The Humboldtian approach consists of two principles. The first considers teaching and research as one unit among the university's functions. The second puts the freedom of the university and its autonomy at the heart of its management, because HEIs should seek knowledge and conduct research according to their own desires and not to serve any other political or religious institution's ideology. Berlin University, created in 1810 by Von Humboldt, maintained its independence from the government and provided an example for other universities in the world to follow (Zimmerman 2005).

From the beginning of the nineteenth century, the model of the teaching and research institution jealous of its autonomy in governance was increasingly embraced by universities (Ferlie et al. 2008). This concept transforms HEIs into autonomous institutions that expect the political authority (government) to limit its intervention in higher education, independent of funding. The provision of funds should not be a means to influence or jeopardize the academic autonomy of HEIs, because public institutions should be able to obtain public funds without sacrificing their right to independently set their own standards (Davidovitch and Iram 2015).

After 1945, governments began to modify their relationship to HEIs, reducing universities' autonomy in matters of governance and thus introducing the concept of accountability (Graham 1989; McLendon 2003). Public universities started competing with the private institutions in terms of collecting funds and attracting new students through developing self-regulatory system, forming boards of trustees and planning the establishments' policies with a clear advantage of a political support over their rivals (McLendon et al. 2007).

This independence of HEIs led to misconduct resulting from an absence of supervision, opening the door to criticism (Amaral 2009). This led to a debate on the need for government intervention in the governance of HEIs, and as a result universities became subject to accountability, accepting government control through evaluation, regulation, and monitoring (King 2007; King et al. 2007). A system of governance that involved a new role for government, aimed at establishing more order and increasing efficiency in the academic environment, was implemented in several countries (McLendon et al. 2007).

The Role of Government

The role of government in higher education has evolved according to changes in political systems and the economic environment. Governments usually justify their interventions to regulate higher education systems based on two economic factors: first, because any government investment in HEIs may result, in the long run, in external benefits due to initiatives in research domains that lead to beneficial technological innovation; and, second, because individuals may be affected by the imperfections of the market and therefore be unable to afford higher education expenses, resulting in social disequilibrium (World Bank 1994).

Indeed, the government role cannot be understood and defined unless we define the exact domain being addressed, which in our case is education. Education is composed of three categories. The first category is educational programs. An educational program is the sum of courses (curricula) that enable students to obtain a degree. Different types of institutions can provide this service, whether they are public or private, owned by a religious institution or by government, profit-making or not, and so on. The second category is educational products, such as textbooks, billboards, copybooks, pedagogical software, and so forth. This category represents about 35% of educational spending (Heyneman 2001). In most socialist societies, this expense was the responsibility of the ministry of education. In developed countries, educational products are supplied by the private sector, responding when necessary—as in the case of textbooks—to the content requirements defined by the government (Heyneman et al. 2007). Education services are the last category of education; this refers primarily to adult learning delivered through training and adult employment. This third category of education is not an obligatory element in HEIs' offerings, and for some theorists it is still a controversial matter, because it is not included in all theoretical definitions of education (Heyneman 2000, 2007).

The role of the government consists in regulating, or in some cases financing, these educational products and services, mainly because they are offered by non-public institutions in an open market, and these institutions have to respect the public regulations regarding these products and services. Thus the role of the government in relation to the educational categories is divided into three functions: providing the programs, financing the products, and regulating. The area in which the government can be seen as intrusive is in the provision of educational programs (Tooley 1996). Some theorists advocate an intrusive role for the state government in supplying, financing, and regulating public institutions, while others would prefer to involve the private sector (Heyneman 2008). The intrusive role of the government can be considered as a social advantage, since it may create social cohesion within a country. It is considered a necessity to ensure social justice and meritocracy through equal and fair access to education. Social justice is necessary to protect democracy. But this policy of intervention has its drawbacks, mainly when it reduces the autonomy of HEIs, because this can have a negative impact on educational innovation. The main question that remains is how to ensure social justice while maintaining the quality of education. Thus, national culture and its values will affect the nature of government intervention in higher education governance, resulting in different models of governance for HEIs. Those new models will positively affect the market as they lead towards highly skilled graduates that will later on join the workforce in both the public and private sector (Clark 1983).

Models of Governance in Higher Education

Governance models are influenced by the interaction of three elements—the market, the government, and academic expertise—and are highly affected by the origins and the history of HEIs (Dobbins and Knill 2014). There are three models to consider: the first gives full authority to the government, the second gives full autonomy to the HEI, and the third is based on continuous adaptation and adjustment to market forces (Dobbins et al. 2011). The state-centered model is too conservative when it comes to regulation. In this model, the government is responsible for coordinating the different aspects of higher education, because HEIs are considered to be public institutions run by the political system. Little autonomy is given to HEIs because they are expected to operate to serve national goals and interests. The government intervenes in all details related to the governance of these institutions, the quality of their services, their relation to the market, their orientation toward specific research topics, and their allocation of resources (Dobbins et al. 2011). This model offers a very solid hierarchy, common legislation for all HEIs across the country, and close relations between universities and the state (Dobbins et al. 2011). The main countries pursuing this model are France, Sweden, Turkey, and Russia (Panova 2008). The self-rule model defines universities as organisms serving the goals of the government. In this model, universities define their own goals and research objectives that carry their own intrinsic values independent of national and social interests (Olsen 2007). HEIs gain more autonomy but lack good connections with market forces and the political system. The countries pursuing this model are mainly those of central Europe, Austria, and Germany (Dobbins et al. 2011). The market-oriented model perceives universities as efficient as a result of good connections with market forces. Adapted to the liberal free market system, universities function as financial corporations that compete among each other in order to attract more students and financial resources. This competitiveness allows universities to deliver better-quality services. In this context government intervention is not appreciated. Its role is to ensure the transparency of the market in order to enhance competition; so, the market will have the greatest influence on the decisions made in the governance of HEIs. The USA (Kirsch 2014) (Adkit, International Information and Research 2014) and Austria (Norton 2012) (Breen 2002) are the best examples of this model.

Arab World: The Government Role in Higher Education Governance

After the Second World War, decolonization gave rise to new independent Arab states that sought economic development and were willing to play the role of welfare state. For these new states, higher education was of great importance in order to gain the political support of the upper middle classes with the aim of centralizing and empowering the state (Mazawi 2005). Graduates were satisfied, since they were immediately employed by the government to teach high school students (Teixeira 2009). In this way, the higher education system enhanced social mobility and ensured the total control of the government over HEIs (Cohen 2004). Two countries were an exception to this rule in the Arab world: Lebanon and Palestine. Both states were suffering from political turmoil. Lebanon's war dislocated the national university and opened the door to the rise of private universities, founded originally by religious groups (Bashshur 2006). In the case of Lebanon, higher education moved away from state control and became decentralized, with more than 60% of Lebanese students enrolling in higher education (Nahas 2009). In Palestine, the higher education system was highly privatized, and HEIs were able to set their own standards and determine their funding away from the control of the state, which was newly born after the Oslo Accords in 1994 (Mazawi 2005; Nakhleh 2006). If there is a lesson to be learned from these two exceptions to higher education governance in the Arab world, it is that political conflicts prevented the state from controlling the higher education system. The best indicator of the positive outcome of universities' autonomy is the expansion of enrollment, and Lebanon and Palestine had the highest enrollment expansion in the Arab world (Schofer and Meyer 2005).

In the rest of the Arab world, we have witnessed in since 2000 an increase in the number of students in higher education. The number of students rose from 2.967 million to 7.607 million in one decade (1998–2008), an acceleration of 256%, while the population grew by only 139%. This increase reflects an expansion in the social demand for higher education (El Amine et al. 2009). The proportion of females in higher education in the Arab world increased as well, to 50% of the total. In some countries (Kuwait, Saudi Arabia, and the United Arab Emirates [UAE]) this rate exceeded 60%, while in others (Iraq and Yemen) it did not exceed 40%. The expansion in enrollment is the result not only of an increase in population, but also of the effect of pressure on the Arab world to liberalize its market, enter the neoliberal economy, and adapt to globalization. Higher education liberalization is included in the GATS (General Agreement on Trades in Services) negotiations that started in January of the year 2000 and concluded on March 2001. The aim of these negotiations was to remove national barriers to trade in services, including higher education. Arab countries that wished to negotiate their admission to the GATS were obliged to open their markets to foreign HEIs, which would increase the competition between local and international universities. This would affect the role of the state in higher education governance, since most Arab states tend toward intervention in higher education governance.

The Role of Government in Funding Determination to Ensure Equal Opportunity

Admissions regulations in the Arab countries are centralized and are based on students' grades in high school, knowing that the socioeconomic background of students could be a major obstacle affecting their enrollment. In order to advance equality and equity, states provide funds to HEIs according to different measures. In Jordan, Royal Donations are granted to students who come from underprivileged areas or social backgrounds. In Tunisia, eight universities are awarded scholarships and loans by the government as social aid to families with low annual incomes; almost 35% of Tunisian students benefit from these scholarships, and 31% of Moroccans students receive such social aid. Oman provides the same programs, which are considered to be a way to help ensure social security. In Kuwait, scholarships are awarded to governmental and non-governmental universities based on the academic performance of students (El Amine et al. 2009).

The Role of Government in Control and Quality Assurance

Several countries in the Arab world have established committees to control and guarantee the quality of education. In Jordan, legislation was introduced in 2007 to create the Higher Education Accreditation Commission (HENC), which has authority over public and non-public universities. In Tunisia, the National Committee of Evaluation was created in June 1993 by a ministerial decision, and in 2006 a new higher education law established the National Commission of Evaluation, Quality Assurance and Accreditation. In Saudi Arabia, the

National Commission for Academic Accreditation and Quality Assurance was created in 2004. In Oman, under the supervision of the Higher Education Council, the Oman Accreditation Council was created. In Egypt, an authority for Accreditation and Quality Assurance was created in 2006 and attached to the prime minister. In other Arab countries, such as Bahrain (Art.9 law 3 of 2005 and decree 32 in 2008), Syria, Iraq, Morocco, and Yemen (El Amine et al. 2009), laws prevent the creation of similar bodies. Government intervention in higher education governance is also reflected through development policies and attempts to reform HEIs using different strategies, plans, projects, and laws. Jordan, Syria, Oman, Lebanon, Egypt, and Yemen established new national strategies for higher education (Jordan, Oman, Lebanon, and Egypt) and to implement new policies (Syria). Other countries established projects to develop a National Notifications Framework (UAE), to promote creativity and excellence (Saudi Arabia), to enhance technical education and reduce emigration (Sudan), to found and equip 23 university campuses (Libya), to develop the infrastructure of higher education (Egypt), and to establish a higher education network to improve the capacity of the ministry of higher education (Yemen). Saudi Arabia prepared a plan to boost different aspects of higher education; at the same time, different countries introduced laws to improve their higher education (Bahrain in 2005), to support the quality of education (Tunisia in 2008), to restructure scientific research and the ministry of higher education (Iraq), to reform the education system (Marcus), and to regulate higher education (Mauritania 2006/2007) (El Amine et al. 2009).

Diversification of HEIs

The increase in the social demand for higher education, and the pressure on Arab states to open up their services in higher education to the free market, have led governments to allow the establishment of new HEIs. These have expanded considerably, mainly those of foreign universities. Western universities were established in the Arab world by colonial powers, primarily European ones, among which the leading nations were France and the UK. They promoted a higher education system that served their own interests and reinforced their control over the Arab world. Before the Second World War, the USA played only a modest role in the Middle East. Missionaries and educators founded the American University of Beirut (AUB) in Lebanon in 1866 and the American University of Cairo (AUC) in Egypt in 1919. These successful enterprises then served as prototypes for the proliferation of similar institutions. Since the year 1958, the USA has witnessed a rejection of its foreign policy because of its support of Israel against the Arab world, in particular Palestine, but controversially, the American style of higher education remained very popular. Arab families were ready to pay high tuition fees for the quality delivered by American HEIs. The establishment of American universities in the Arab world also led to the migration of Arab students abroad. American universities were established in several Arab countries: Egypt, the UAE, Lebanon, Kuwait, and Jordan. An education city in Qatar included branches of the best American universities. American HEIs delivered better educational services and products promoting critical thinking and using interactive methods. In Jordan, there is a branch of the New York Institute of Technology, and Al-Zaytoonah University is affiliated with the Nebraska College of Nursing. In Kuwait, there are ten American institutions for higher education. Because there is a law in Kuwait that segregates education in both public and private universities, the government and parliament intervened to urge private institutions to implement that law.

In Morocco, the fees charged by HEIs make it almost impossible for some social classes to access American universities, which decreases social justice and meritocracy. Qatar is attracting branches of the most prestigious universities in the USA. In Saudi Arabia, the close connection between education and Islam means that conformity of the curriculum to Islamic law and respect for gender segregation are essential. Nevertheless, there are a number of English-language universities and colleges in Saudi Arabia. In Syria, most higher education is provided by the state. However, legislation was introduced in 2001 to allow the establishment of foreign universities in the country (El Amine et al. 2009).

The introduction of Western universities into the Arab world has been problematic for several reasons. On the educational level, the foreign curricula that are imported are not in harmony with the national sociocultural contexts. This goes against one of the main objectives of higher education, which is to protect and to promote national culture. On the sociocultural level, the mission of higher education is not only to serve economic and/or professional purposes; it is about promoting cultural values and enhancing social equality. Foreign universities are focused primarily on economic profitability and typically neglect the national culture of the host country.

This dichotomy between the supposed objectives of higher education governance and the technical tools showed many new challenges related to the new government role in higher education governance in the Arab world. Effectively, instead of perceiving the government as having a positive role, most of the analysis shows a negative perception of its increasing interference.

Perceptions of the Government Role

Government is considered effective in its new role in higher education governance when it avoids direct control and uses public resources efficiently. A positive government role is to establish reforms through a clear definition of policies, to search for practical instruments with which to implement these policies, and to give greater autonomy to public institutions (World Bank 1994).

In terms of the policy framework, it should be coherent and articulate in the long term, employing a legal framework as a guide for consistent policies linked to the national culture and other conditions. In the Arab world, there is a lack of long-term policies aligned with national conditions. The governance of higher education is endowed with high state expenditures, but it is pursued without regard for the cultural and national environment. Such mechanistic planning can achieve a positive outcome on a quantitative level, creating a better image of the central political authority, but this approach rarely achieves real targets in long-term development, mainly because decision-makers are not involved in a consensus process and are excluded from any dynamic participation in the overall political process in the countries concerned (World Bank 1994). Despite the efforts made in the Arab world to establish bodies that are responsible for quality assurance and performance, these bodies are still linked directly to governments and therefore lack independence. Budget allocations for education curricula are related to feedback from the market. People are generally skeptical of the government's role higher education in the Arab world. Most universities in the Arab world are still government institutions dependent on government support both financially and administratively. The academic status, quality, and efficiency of HEIs are not improving in line with expectations due to rigid regimes that are afraid of losing control and are thus incapable of liberating themselves completely from the system. The lack of participation in decision-making leads to a lack of realistic analysis of educational institutions and creates inadequate practices that enlarge the gap between HEIs and market forces. All these factors diminish the academic status of HEIs and limit scholarly innovation (Ali Al-Rashdan 2009).

Furthermore, the centralized bureaucratic structure of the HEIs reflects the overall political system. More than 95% of educational decisions made by educational institutions are controlled by governments and specifically by the ministry of education. This type of centralized state model, with its lack of transparency, negatively affects HEIs' ability to innovate and significantly reduces the capacity for innovation in the domain of research and development. Such a situation explains the poor contribution of Arab universities to the production of knowledge, especially in the fields of science and technology, patents, and other domains affecting the position of Arab universities in rankings of universities worldwide. This perception of the government role paints a negative picture and reveals a legal exception in terms of higher education governance in the Arab World when compared to international HEIs. The governance structures are still unable to adopt the changes in the field. Rigid public policies; absence of autonomy from the political system; lack of responsiveness to the needs of universities, faculties, and students; maladjustment to market forces; and bureaucracies' inability to implement reforms if legislated are negatively affected by the good policies of higher education governance. Accountability of educational agents is delegated to government authorities. In most Arab countries, presidents of public universities are appointed by the political authority; in private universities, if governments do not directly nominate university presidents, they can indirectly affect their nomination and their policymaking. Even student admissions and enrollment are centrally managed by political authorities (Wilkens 2011). The higher education system in the Arab world, despite all the efforts and government expenditure to improve higher education governance, reflects a deeper level of challenges and problems. It is not only about increasing the amount of capital invested in HEIs, nor about the technical elements and tools needed to improve the governance of HEIs; it is more about the nature of the relationship that should exist between governance and democracy in theory and practice. A system of higher education governance that promotes critical thinking and national culture requires an environment of democratic culture and a democratic political system in order to flourish.

Higher Education Governance and Democracy in the Arab World

HEIs are simultaneously agents of change and innovation on the one hand, and agents for the preservation of social tradition on the other hand. This is why HEIs are directly linked to the sociopolitical environment: They are impregnated by sociocultural values, and they prevent change in accordance with these values. Thus, given this relationship between the sociopolitical environment and educational institutions, HEIs become the platform of intersection between the ultimate public and private objectives of a society; one of their duties is to promote a meritocratic civil society. HEIs are invited to spread more inclusive values related to the public interest rather than to religious communities or other components of society. These inclusive values are related to social norms, as open debate and rational and critical thinking encourage students to rely on themselves and to develop their autonomy and self-worth as individuals. Education based on such values rejects any form of discrimination related to religious belief or gender or other types of discrimination. HEIs are the best organizations to build a modern civil society. Furthermore, a modern civil society cannot be established outside of a democratic political system promoting pluralism and accountability. Such an educational system cannot succeed without research in social sciences facilitating the understanding of the society in order to enhance citizenship and produce enlightened citizens. These citizens can contribute to the proliferation of the values of tolerance, freedom, and free thinking. These values can enhance democracy, but cannot be implemented easily outside of a democratic system (The Task Force on Higher Education and Society 2000).

In most of the Arab world, political regimes are either kingdoms, which base their legitimacy on religious values that are directly inspired by Islamic laws; pseudo-republic systems that mask dictatorship, where presidents win fake democratic elections with 99% of the vote; or religious totalitarian regimes that apply Islamic law directly. In such political systems, autonomy and free thinking may appear to governments to be a threat to their authority and a suspicious activity that needs to be contained. The control of universities and continuous intervention in higher education governance become a main focus of interest that is no less important than the control of audio-visual institutions and social media. At the same time, the historical practice of regimes oppressing their societies after the end of the Second World War created societies with a cultural submissiveness, which was a defense mechanism practiced by individuals and the elite as a way to ensure physical security. One of the main fields in higher education that is capable of developing free-thinking citizens is the teaching of a society's shared memory through history. Even when memories are painful, the discussion and the debate of such history may be the right tool to liberate individuals from the burden of the past in order to prepare and build a better future; HEIs are the right place to produce shared memory, to purify it of emotional responses, and to transform it from an unconscious negative element to a conscious positive factor in preparing for the future. Such reflection may even be inspiring to the curriculum of civic education and history in pre-university studies. The shared memory in the Arab world is still an official story told and controlled by the political authority. This means that the social culture in the Arab world is not prepared to implement authentic higher education governance. Such an implementation will not succeed due to the lack of free discourse, free searching, and tolerance that are under direct control by the government and the bureaucratic system. Indeed, in the Arab world, the rigidity of bureaucratic systems and the religious ideology of the governments and political regimes, whether declared or hidden, are an obstacle to the implementation of a real higher education governance system. This explains the continuous intervention of governments in the details of the higher education system, as they consider HEIs agents for the consolidation of their position and aim to have an elite that is completely submissive to the political system and to its perpetuation.

This highlights the problems inherent in implementing higher education governance in the Arab world. Education institutions naturally reflect their societies, which they aim to serve. Developing countries, including those in the Arab world, find it difficult to promote a participative governance approach to higher education because they lack the democratic tools needed for such an approach. In such cases, undemocratic countries, even those with the will to improve higher education governance, end up encountering change as a result of external factors. Politicians have the tendency to increase their intervention in higher education institutions, as any form of independence developed by such institutions is considered to be a political threat. Indeed, the rise of political Islam in the Arab World since 2001 may be partly the outcome of the educational system failing to address the contradiction between the extremists' Islamist values and the objectives of a higher education system. Such a contradiction can explain many of the imperfections and obstacles encountered in the implementation of a system of higher education governance, such as the appointment of people who are affiliated with the government instead of priority being based on merit. With time, unqualified people will run the education system, diminishing the quality of education even though commissions and bodies for quality assurance might be increasing in number. The diversification of HEIs and the internationalization of education—mostly following the American model of education, which is valued in the Arab world—may appear to be a way to modernize higher education governance and to establish international standards that improve the whole educational system. This may be the case, but it still raises two problematic issues.

First, as a result of political instability and, in some countries, the turmoil and clashes that have escalated to the level of war, especially since the Arab Spring, American visiting professors are more likely to teach courses for a few weeks instead of remaining for longer periods in host countries. Another reason for this situation is the inadequate nature of the social and cultural environment in host countries for families and children of professors who come from Western societies.

This reality negatively affects the sharing of information and experience between Western professors and local teachers; it diminishes the capacity to communicate on HEIs' governance systems and to empower such systems by drawing on the personnel of the universities in the host countries. Competencies in governing the higher education system will continue to be dependent on Western intervention instead of being filled by personnel from all levels of the administration and teaching staff; changes in the higher education system will be cyclical and accidental instead of being permanent and sustainable.

Second, the international universities established in the Arab world may be a source of inequity and social injustice. Since the tuition fees of international universities are, for the most part, higher than the local ones, underprivileged members of society are unable to attend these universities, and only students from posh sectors of society will be able to pursue a high level of education. The students who attend these universities usually come from the families of political officers or upper-class families who are affiliated with the political regime. Students who receive their education in Western universities are more likely to access the best opportunities in the labor market. This maintains the gap between social classes and reinforces social injustice and inequity.

Conclusion

The role of government in higher education governance in the Arab world is a complex issue. Historically, higher education institutions were founded by religious groups affiliated with political authorities. During the colonial period, the established universities served the interests of colonial governments instead of the interests of Arab societies. After the Second World War, the newly independent Arab countries—dictatorships, theocratic regimes, or kingdoms based on Islamic law—perceived HEIs as a means to consolidate their authority and to align the rising elite with the interests of the political regime. A long tradition of government control over the higher education system influenced the model of higher education governance. After the collapse of the Soviet Union, and with the pressure of globalization and the increasing unemployment rate in the Arab world, the higher education system in the Arab world faced new challenges. Rapid population growth increased the social demand for higher education and resulted in the foundation of new universities and the diversification of HEIs. The Arab world opened its doors to Western universities, mainly American ones. Despite increases in the budgets given to HEIs, funding remained insufficient, failing to cover the growing needs of universities.

The government role in higher education governance is essential, because the government has almost full control over the higher education sector. Government intervention is applied through funding, laws, project planning, established policies, social aids to secure equal opportunities, creation of commissions and bodies to ensure quality control and quality assurance, and opening up of the local market to foreign institutions supplying educational services. Sometimes the intervention goes beyond the global legal framework, and governments intervene by appointing universities' presidents and deans or by centralizing the process of student enrollment.

As much as government intervention can help to improve the higher education system, the drawbacks can be significant. An excess of control limits academic freedom, such as open debates, free expression, and exchange of opinions; in addition, a lack of clear policies and a small budget dedicated to research leads to low-quality production in this domain. Gender discrimination is decreasing, although the gender segregation that is protected by law remains. Governance of HEIs remains tightly linked to the government, with little autonomy given to universities and an almost total absence of participative or shared decision-making. The main problem with the government role affecting the higher education system lies in the inadequate connection between the local culture and the type of higher education governance system that is employed, which is inspired by the values of governance types that flourished in Western societies as a reflection of their own cultures. In order to develop an efficient governance system, more democratization of the Arab world is needed in order to provide universities with greater autonomy and to give actors more involvement in decision-making at all levels.

References

Adkit, International Information and Research (2014). *Higher education – regulatory models in the world.* Jerusalem: International Review.

Ali Al-Rashdan, A.-F (2009, Winter). Higher education in the Arab world: Hopes and challenges. *Arab Insight,* 109.

Amaral, A. (2009, January). Recent trends in European higher education. In *Reforms and consequences in higher education systems: An international symposium.* Tokyo: Center for National Finance and Management.

Bashshur, M. (2006). Standards of quality of higher education in Lebanon. In Y. C. M. Bashshur (Ed.), *L'enseignement supérieur dans le monde arabe: une question de niveau? Higher education in the Arab world: A question of level?].* Beirut: Institut Français du Proche Orient (French Institute of the Near East).

Boer, H., and File, J. (2009). *Higher education governance reforms across Europe.* Brussels: Center for Higher Education Policy Studies (CHEPS).

Bowman, M. J. (1962). The land grant colleges and Universities in human resource development. *Journal of Economic History, 22*(04), 523–546.

Breen, J. (2002). *Higher education in Australia: Structure, policy and debate.* Amhurst, MA: Monash University.

Clark, B. R. (1983). *The higher education system.* Berkeley: University of California Press.

Cobban, A (1992). Reflections on the role of medievel universities in soceity. In Smith B. Ward (Eds.), *Intellectual life in the middle ages.* London: Hambeldon Press.

Cohen, S. (2004). *Searching for a different future: The rise of a global middle class in Morocco.* Durham, NC: Duke University Press.

Corcoran, S. (2004). Duty, discretion and conflict: University governance and the legal obligations of unversity boards. *Australian Universities Review, 46*(2), 30.

Davidovitch, N. Iram (2015). Models of higher education governance: A comparison of Israel and other countries. *Global Journal of Educational Studies, 1*(1), 16.

Dobbins, M., Knill, C., and Vögtle, E. M. (2011). An analytical framework for the cross-country comparison of higher education governance. *Higher Education,* 62.

Dobbins, M., and Knill, C. (2014). *Higher education governance and policy change in Western Europe: International challenges to historical institutions.* Hampshire: Palgrave Macmillan.

El Amine, A., Abou Rjeili, K., Hoteit, S., Dick, M., Bashur, M., Al Awit, H., and Lamine, B. (2009). *A decade of higher education in the Arab states: Achievements and challenges.* Beirut—Lebanon: UNESCO Regional Bureau for Education in the Arab States.

Ferlie, E., Musselin, C., and Andresani, G. (2008). The steering of higher education systems: A public management perspective. *Higher Education, 56*(3), 325–348.

Glenn, C. (1988). *The myth of the common school.* Amherst, MA: University of Massachusetts Press.

Graham, H. (1989). Structure and governance in American higher educution: Historical and comparative analysis in state policy. *Journal of Policy History, 1*(1), 80–107.

Haskins, C. H. (1957). *The rise of universities.* Ithaca, NY: Cornell University Press.

Helmreich, E. (1959). *Christian religious education in German schools: An historical approach.* Cambridge, MA: Harvard University Press.

Heynemam (1997). Education and Social Stabilization In Russia. *Compare,* 27.

Heyneman, S. (2008). *International Perspectives on school choice.* Mark Berends, Mathew G. Springer, Dale Ballou, and Herbert Wlberg (Eds.) New Jersey: Lawrence Erlbaum Publishers.

Heyneman, S. P. (2001). The growing international market for education goods and services. *International Journal of Education Development*, *21*, 345–361.

Heyneman, S. P. (2000, November). Educational Qualifications: The economic and trade issues. *Assessment in Education: Principles, Policy and Practice*, A. Little (Ed.), Special issue on globalization, qualifications and livelihoods, *7*(3), 64–68.

Heyneman, S. P. (2007). International trade in higher education: What should india do. *The India Economic Review*, *4*(4), 86–93.

Heyneman, S. P., Anderson, K. H., and Nuraliyeva, N. (2007). The cost of corruption in higher education. *Comparative Education Review*, *52*(1), 1–25.

Hyman, H. H., and Wright, C.R. (1979). *Education's lasting impact on values.* Chicago: University of Chicago Press.

Hyneman, S. (1995). *Education in the Europe and central Asia region: Policies of adjusment and excellence.* Washington, DC: World Mertons (ed).

King, R., Griffiths, P., and Williams, R. (2007). Regulatory intermediation and quality assurance in higher education: The case of the auditors. *Oxford Review of Education*, *33*(2), 161–174.

King, R. P. (2007). Governance and accountability in the higher education regulatory state. *Higher Education*, 53.

Kirsch, U (2014). *The higher education system in Israel – Issues, characteristics, and unique aspects.* Jerusalem: Shmuel Ne'aman Institute.

Mazawi, A. E. (2005). *Contrasting Perspectives on Higher Education in the Arab States.* In J. Smart (Ed.), *Higher education: handbook of theory and research.* (Vol. XX). London: Springer.

McLendon, M. (2003). *State governance reform of higher education: Patterns, trends, and theories of the public policy process..* In J. C Smart (Ed.), *Higher education: Handbook of theory and research* (Vol. XVIII). Netherlands: Springer.

McLendon, M. K., Deaton, R., and Hearn, J. C. (2007). The enactment of reforms in state governance of higher education: Testing the political instability hypothesis. *The Journal of Higher Education*, *78*(6), 645–675.

Nahas, C. (2009). *Financing and political economy of higher education in Lebanon.* Cairo, Egypt: Economic Research Forum.

Nakhleh, K. (2006). Palestinian Tertiary Educational System: Overview, Challenges and Possible Responses. In *L'enseignement supérieur dans le monde arabe: une question de niveau? [Higher education in the arab world: A question of Lev-el?].* (Y. C. ed. M. Bashshur, Ed.). Beirut: Institut Français du Proche-Orient (French Institute of the Near East).

Neave, G. (2003). The Bolgna Decleration: Some of the historic dilemmas posed by the reconstruction of the community in Europe's systems of higher education. *Educational Policy.*

Norton, A. (2012). *Mapping Australian higher education.* Carlton, VIC: Grattan.

Olsen, J. (2007). The institutional dynamics of the European University. In M Peter and O. Johan (Eds.), *University dynamics and European integration.* Dordrecht: Springer.

Panova, A. (2008). Governance structures and decision making in Russian higher education institutions. *Problems of Economic Transition, 50*(10), 65–82.

Perkins, H. (1984). *The Historical Perspective. Perspectives on higher education. Eight disciplinary and comparative views,* 17–55. Berkley: University of California Press.

Readings, B. (1996). *The university in ruins.* Cambradge, MA: Harvard University Press.

Rowlands, J. (2013). Academic Board: Less Intellectual and more academic capital in higher education governance? *Studies in Higher Education, 38*(9), 1274–1289.

Schechter, S. (2006). *Crocks in the ivory Tower.* Jerusalem: Tzivonim.

Schofer, E., and Meyer, J. W. (2005). The worldwide expansion of higher education in the twentieth century. *American sociological review, 70*(6), 898–920.

Scott, J. C. (2006). The mission of the university: Mediaval to postmodern transformations. *Journal of Higher Education, 77*(1), 1–39.

Teixeira, P. (2009). *Mass higher education and private institute in higher education to 2030: Globalization.* (Vol. 2). Paris: Center for Educational Research and Innovation, OECD.

The Task Force on Higher Education and Society (2000). *Higher education in developing countries peril and promise.* Washington, DC: The International Bank for Reconstruction and Development /The World Bank.

Tooley, J. (1996). Education without the State. *Institute of Economic Studies.*

Wilkens, K. (2011). Higher Education Reform in the Arab World. The Brookings Project on US Relations with the Islamic World. 2011 US-Islamic World Forum Papers. Brookings Institution.

World Bank, S (1994). *Higher education: The lessons of experience.* Washington, DC: Library of Congress.

Zimmerman (2005). Concept of the university, science, and the state from a historical perspective. In A. Gur Zeev (Ed.), *End of Israel's academia?* Haifa: Haifa University, Department of Education.

Antoine Habchi is an Associate Professor at the Faculty of Business and Commercial Sciences at USEK. He founded the Middle East Institute for Research and Strategic Studies, an NGO involved in the publication of analytical reports and the preparation of round-table debates. He is also founder of CHAINGE Consulting, a firm specializing in tailoring customized training programs and tackling managerial problems facing both private and public organizations. The Central Bank of Lebanon, the Association of Banks in Lebanon, and the Rosary School of Byblos are among the many organizations for which he has provided both training and consulting. He also founded the Hotel Management department "L.T. Hotellerie" at Cortbawi Institute and has managed the Organizational Project of Aintoura College along with several educational institutions.

Educational Reform, Privatization, and the Challenge of Collaborative Governance in Higher Education in the Arab World

John Willoughby

Introduction

The education of youth plays a key role in the reproduction of social norms and institutions and the maintenance of our material well-being. The educational experience lies at the center of what it means to be human in the modern world. A key purpose of formal education is to facilitate the transmission and production of knowledge by training students in the art of logical reasoning. Well-functioning systems of education encourage the empirically grounded, rigorous, and creative use of symbolic discourse so that we can discover new understandings of the material and cultural worlds that we are constantly recreating and changing.

The educational process requires well-trained teachers who not only have solid training in the knowledge they are transmitting but can creatively interact with and inspire their students. This is true at

J. Willoughby (✉)
American University, Washington, DC, USA
e-mail: jwillou@american.edu

G. Azzi (ed.), *Higher Education Governance in the Arab World*,
DOI 10.1007/978-3-319-52060-5_7

131

all levels of instruction, but teachers of more advanced students require more opportunities to experiment and explore. This is because the findings that need to be communicated to students are less settled, and students themselves must learn how to use creatively the methods of reasoning and empirical investigations they are learning. This openness has led higher education institutions (HEIs) to have a higher-than-normal commitment to open-mindedness and a greater tolerance for dissident views. It is not a coincidence that the most prestigious universities are often sources of destabilizing scientific and political ideas. For professors, such zones of liberal discourse are often protected by a meritocratic tenure system that is under the control of the most advanced and senior scholars of the institution. Even in countries where tenure is not allowed, it is nonetheless the case that academics often enjoy much more job security and more unstructured work time than professionals in other enterprises. This system has important implications for the ways in which the higher education enterprise should be managed or governed.

In this chapter, we argue that the best-functioning HEIs practice a collaborative form of governance that cedes considerable power to academic workers to manage the instructional and research missions of the college or university. This type of joint management is outlined and described in more detail in the next section of the chapter. This finding has implications for the ways in which ownership relations affect governance. On the one hand, public ownership might prevent an HEI from establishing the political autonomy from state authorities that is necessary for the proper functioning of the establishment. On the other hand, profit-driven privatization might lead to a more hierarchical management system that also challenges faculty autonomy.

These issues are explored in more depth in the following section. After these general propositions on governance and ownership have been established, the chapter examines how the wave of privatization within the higher education system of Gulf Cooperation Council (GCC) countries has affected the governance of these new institutions (Badry and Willoughby 2015). We argue that privatization can promote a more liberal form of governance for universities and colleges, but this is not guaranteed. What is more important is the general mission or goals of the university's or college's ownership group.

Why Collaborative Governance in HEIs?

The standard justification for job security and collaborative governance among faculty is, as we noted in the introduction, the need to protect the creative work of academics and promote relatively free intellectual discourse. This is, indeed, an important part of the explanation for this unique system of enterprise management, but there are other factors at play as well.

Most academics do not take students to the frontiers of knowledge, and the majority of professors are not engaged in state-of-the-art research. Some high-profile institutions in the USA have recognized this, and have developed a two-tier professoriate in which a sizeable number of faculty are contingently employed on limited contracts, while others are granted job security and reductions in teaching obligations in order to produce research that will bring prestige to the HEIs. This type of system permits university administrators who are, by and large, no longer engaged directly in academic work to establish more control over the workplace, since the less privileged academic workers are not likely to challenge administration prerogatives, and the more privileged already have sufficient protection.

Nevertheless, even when this hierarchical and differentiated system is established, the evidence suggests that most HEIs continue to rely on collaborative governance. In most well-run universities, a subset of college instructors work actively on committees to preserve and improve the curricula while establishing standards for the awarding of degrees; senior faculty in academic departments still evaluate the work of junior colleagues and determine who might be eligible for tenure or longer-term job security; and all instructors still autonomously evaluate and award students with minimal interference from higher-level administrators.

What are the other factors responsible for this broad-based delegation of responsibilities to "shop-floor" workers? We would argue that there are three major reasons for the existence of higher educational enterprises whose core mission (teaching and research) is organized and operated by the workers themselves. First, higher education administrators cannot easily observe and evaluate the research and teaching work of academics. Second, it is not easy to replace individual university professors without disrupting the work of academic departments. And third, the workers themselves are trained in and learn to embrace a meritocratic workplace culture in which one's standing as a prestigious worker is not determined by one's administrators but rather by academics in other institutions. These monitoring, substitutability, and cultural issues mean that it makes sense for administrators to allow the establishment of a workplace that encourages academic workers to establish and monitor their own work within the context of generally recognized academic standards. (For a more general discussion of the economics of enterprise governance, see Williamson 1996.)

This system of governance should not be confused with worker self-management. In all cases, professors work within a larger institution that grants significant power to allocate resources to the president or chancellor of the college or university. In addition, student affairs, the development and maintenance of facilities, financial management, and human resource management are normally the province of a professional and non-professional workforce separated from the faculty and subject to more traditional forms of command and control.

Because of this unique, heterogeneous management structure, the governance of colleges and universities sometimes becomes a political issue. Business and government leaders often suggest that HEIs should be operated more like commercial enterprises because they incorrectly assume there is no significant difference between the higher education enterprise and the more traditional capitalist firm. Moreover, government leaders and other economic and cultural elites sometimes desire to discipline dissident voices in such a way that academic freedom and workplace autonomy is significantly eroded.

Governance and the Privatization of Universities and Colleges: The Case of the GCC

The preceding analysis suggests that the governance of universities and colleges should be relatively similar. Whether or not an institution is publicly funded or privately owned, and whether or not the political practices of a country are authoritarian or democratic, the needs of HEIs require some, but not unlimited, faculty autonomy.

This does not mean that political systems and ownership relations have no impact on governance systems and faculty autonomy within higher education establishments. Anyone who has worked in colleges or universities in the Middle East knows there are certain subjects, such as political leadership and religion, that are best avoided. Moreover, it is plausible to hypothesize that ownership forms might have some unpredictable impact on systems of governance. On the one hand, some have suggested that a move away from public universities should provide more space for faculty experimentation in teaching and research. On the other hand, critics have also complained that privatization can lead to an excessive concern for profit or net revenue maximization, which creates onerous working conditions for faculty that restrict the openness and autonomy to which professors are accustomed.

The GCC nations provide us with an interesting set of cases that allows us to explore this issue. Since 1995, there has been a radical restructuring of higher education in all Gulf states. This has been characterized by a sharp rise in the number of students enrolled in universities and colleges, the rapid growth of a private for-profit and nonprofit higher education sector, the creation of high-prestige branches of Western campuses in a few of the GCC countries, and attempts to restructure the curricula and academic practices of the older public universities. Not only has the size of the student body increased impressively, but its composition has also changed. Non-national students (many of whom are children of expatriate professionals) can now receive college degrees within the GCC, and the number of women in HEIs is now higher than that of men. Although higher education reform has affected all GCC countries (including Saudi Arabia), the nature of the reform process is quite different from country to country. While this is not the place to explore these differences in great detail, our recent book, *Higher Education Revolutions in the Gulf*, chronicles the distinctly different regulatory systems that have been established in each GCC country (Badry and Willoughby 2015).

In order to examine the impact of these reforms on faculty governance, it is first necessary to explain in more detail the new types of HEIs that have emerged in the Arabian Peninsula. We would argue that there are five major categories of colleges and universities in the region:

- relatively small for-profit institutions that focus on providing instruction in business and information technology;
- for-profit and nonprofit institutions that attempt to create larger liberal arts universities with a diversified curricula;
- branch campuses established by a variety of colleges and universities from outside the region, which offer a narrow set of degree programs;
- branch campuses that attempt to establish a diversified liberal arts curriculum as well as prestigious degree programs;
- reformed public universities that have attempted to Westernize and anglicize their curricula and instruction.

How do governance and faculty autonomy differ among these types of establishments?

Private Business and Information Technology Colleges

The creation of business- and information-technology-oriented colleges and universities has met the demand of families who work in the region and wish to have their sons and daughters focus on practical degrees. In countries such as Oman and Bahrain, a significant proportion of the new colleges and universities that have emerged are owned by a single businessman or a small ownership group from the country. In these cases, the evidence suggests that faculty autonomy and governance of the institution by academics is significantly restricted.

This is because the profitability goals of the ownership group can lead to a significant decline in the quality of students admitted to the college; an increase in class size; increased teaching loads; and courses whose content and evaluation procedures are closely monitored. These problems of quality control are often exacerbated in these "diploma mills" by attempts to teach in English despite students lacking the ability or training to engage in higher-order reasoning in this language. Such colleges have often had difficulty receiving final accreditation and instead rely on interim reports that permit the college to continue functioning while working to change its practices. One signal that ownership can matter for these smaller institutions is the insistence of accreditation boards that a separate board of trustees be established to supervise the management of the college. This board is supposed to have members who are well known in the community but who are not financially linked to the owner.[1]

Liberal Arts Colleges and Universities

The more ambitious private liberal arts institutions established in the region have adopted a variety of private ownership forms. These range from for-profit institutions with a clearly identified owner, for-profit institutions established by a more broadly based business group, and nonprofit institutions that often have close ties to business owners or members of the ruling family (often including the ruler himself).[2]

---

[1] Important information on the problems of governance can be gleaned by examining accreditation reports published online by the government of Oman's Oman Academic Accreditation Authority and the government of Bahrain's National Authority for Qualifications and Quality Assurance of Education and Training. See respectively http://www.oaaa.gov.om and http://www.qqa.edu.bh.

[2] Four major institutions that fall into these categories are the Gulf University for Science and Technology (in Kuwait), the American University of Kuwait, the University of Wollongong in Dubai, and the American University of Sharjah (AUS). The case of AUS also demonstrates that it is often difficult to distinguish between private and public universities, since the institution has

Our previous analysis suggests that the establishment of diversified academic programs within one educational institution would require a significant delegation of authority to academic administrators and the professoriate. And indeed, this is what has by and large happened. Deans of colleges are given significant administrative power to hire and replace members of the teaching staff and to supervise and develop the degree programs of a variety of departments. This, in turn, has generally required some of the senior academics to play an important role in committees that oversee curricula and evaluate the academic performance of fellow academic colleagues. In general, these faculty draw on Western practices with which they are familiar.

Not all colleges and universities are identical. Only a few institutions in the GCC have a functioning faculty senate that is able to work with college administrators as well as challenge some administrative decisions. More common is a less inclusive hierarchical structure under the control of senior academic officers. Moreover, one employment regulation that limits academic governance in the GCC is the general prohibition of tenure for expatriate workers. A good number of the more established liberal arts colleges have created a system of rolling contracts to mitigate this problem, but job insecurity is a reality for nearly all expatriate faculty.[3]

Elite Branch Campuses

Another category of non-state or private HEIs that has emerged in the Gulf and attracted the most international attention is elite branch campuses sponsored by prestigious Western institutions based in the USA, the UK, and France. The most well known of these institutions have been established in Qatar and Abu Dhabi. In the case of Qatar, the branch campuses are located in an Education City complex. Each

---

been established as a nonprofit institution but receives significant backing from the ruler of Sharjah.

[3] A rolling contract exists when a faculty member is given a long-term contract of, for example, three years, and then is evaluated for extension in the second year of her or his employment.

American university has signed a contract with the Qatar Foundation and promised to create a specific degree program that is formally identical to the degree program of the home institution. Because most of the degree programs are offered to undergraduates, each university must also provide the liberal arts general education requirements to its students. New York University and the Sorbonne have made similar agreements with the government of Abu Dhabi in the United Arab Emirates (UAE), although both universities offer a more diversified set of degree programs for their students.

The contracts that provide the framework for branch campus operations (especially in the case of Qatar) would suggest that there is little scope for decentralized governance and management, since the curriculum cannot be different from that of the home institution. In fact, our site visits to these campuses revealed a significant delegation of authority to the administrators and faculty of these campuses. Both the different pedagogical challenges and the distinct research opportunities inevitably separate the branch campus from the far-distant home campus.[4] Thus, we observed the emergence of formal and informal systems of governance that are very similar to the free-standing liberal arts universities and colleges in the rest of the region. Indeed, the faculty might be more empowered in these elite branch campuses because home administrators are more used to delegating authority and encouraging more collaboration across ranks of professors.

Non-Elite Branch Campuses

This finding does not apply to the larger number of non-elite branch campuses that have recently been established in the GCC. These institutions, many of which are based in the Dubai Free Trade Zones called Knowledge Village and International Academic City, are often similar to

---

[4] For example, the Georgetown University School of Foreign Service in Qatar has established an impressive Center for International and Regional Studies that has developed a significant publication record in a short period of time.

the for-profit business and information technology colleges we described earlier. In some cases, the institutions offer a single graduate program that employs only one or two professors. In these cases, there are fewer complex governance programs and it is possible for the home institution to establish more centralized administrative control.

Governance in Reformed Public Universities

Perhaps the most interesting cases associated with governance and higher educational reforms can be found in the public sector. The initial decisions to permit the establishment of private universities were based on two factors: the need to expand the higher education system rapidly in order to service the burgeoning number of young adult children from professional expatriate families, and the desire to modernize and improve higher education so that the GCC could play an active role in the global knowledge economy.

The public universities were seen as a hindrance to this modernization project. In the first place, the student body was restricted to national citizens, who for a variety of straightforward economic (not cultural) reasons were less likely to be active participants in a knowledge-based private sector. In addition, however, early critics of the public universities focused on their bureaucratic governance and lack of innovation (Ghabra 2010). The universities lacked financial autonomy, and many of their academic staff came from other Arab countries and were less likely to take risks that might endanger their employment.

In Qatar and the UAE, the result of this perceived crisis was the replacement of Arab administrators with American and British imports. This was linked to the rapid switch to an English-language curriculum for many disciplines and the hiring of Western-trained academics. This top-down process linked modernization to a decline in faculty governance, as new innovations continued to be ordered from "on high." In Qatar's case, the restructuring of Qatar University was organized by high-paid consultants from the RAND Corporation who established a branch office in Education City. The consultants—with the support of

Sheikha Mozah bint Nasser al Missned, head of the Qatar Foundation and wife of the former ruler—used shock-and-awe techniques to remove recalcitrant administrators and rapidly introduce new academic practices (Moini et al. 2009). The process in Abu Dhabi was orchestrated by the long-serving Minister of Higher Education Sheikh Nahyan bin Mubarak Al Nahyan. He used an advisory group based in the USA to hire top administrators for the University of the United Arab Emirates (Al-Ain) and Zayed University. Unfortunately, difficulties in resolving issues of financial and administrative autonomy meant that the expatriate administrators were never able to establish their own systems of sustained governance.

In both the Qatar and UAE cases, the reform of public universities was not associated with the establishment of an appropriate decentralized governance structure that characterizes most high-quality HEIs. In part this was because the reforms themselves were not universally popular with the constituents of parents and students, who were alienated from administrators who could not directly communicate with them. Much of the pre-existing faculty also found themselves in a difficult position, helping parachuted administrators adjust to a very different environment while having to respond to erratic changes in educational priorities and practices that sometimes threatened their own interests. In these two cases, one could argue that state ownership of higher education never completely succeeded in establishing a sustainable higher education system, and, indeed, since 2012 there has been a somewhat disorganized retreat from the Westernizing impulses of the early years of this century (Badry and Willoughby 2015).

The Role of International Accreditation Bodies in the Establishment of Governance Systems within HEIs

Although our focus has been on the ways in which the work process required of academics plays a crucial role in maintaining a relatively collaborative and participatory work culture in colleges and universities, there is also an important global context that influences higher educational governance. There are two important international factors that affect how universities and colleges operate. First, nearly all members of the faculty are trained in the context of a similar academic culture that stresses the importance of meritocratic review of one's work, the irrelevance of national borders in the sharing and development of knowledge, and the free sharing of information. These commitments are not always honored, and many contemporary critics of higher education argue that commercialization is eroding this global framework for maintaining academic excellence. Nevertheless, it is still the case that faculty members are unusually sensitive to the judgment of their peers throughout the world, and they expect the institutions in which they work to reflect this academic culture.

These expectations are backed up by a second factor that has become increasingly important in recent years: the influence of international accreditation agencies. With the exception of Qatar, all GCC countries have strengthened their higher education regulatory bodies by affiliating with the International Network for Quality Assurance Agencies in Higher Education. The practical impact of this alliance has been that regulatory practices have become uniform. Universities and colleges must be recognized and certified by a national regulatory body within the ministries of higher education, and these require a rigorous self-evaluation of the institution's financial and academic viability and site visits from outside experts who are not affiliated with the institution. The reports of these auditors are crucial to receiving certification, and this places constant pressure on non-compliant higher educational establishments that fail to meet basic academic standards. In all cases, some attention is paid to the governance of the institution, especially with regard to the setting of academic standards, the design of curricula, and the assessment of students. Such supervision places pressure on educational establishments that do not comply with international standards. In countries such as Bahrain, Oman, Kuwait, and the UAE, there is good evidence that regulatory interventions restrict the ability of some for-profit colleges to evade rules that limit the intake of unqualified students and the implementation of strict, tyrannical controls over the faculty (Badry and Willoughby 2015).

General Propositions about Privatization and the Governance of HEIs in the Arab World

The GCC experience provides us with interesting insights about the interaction between the governance of HEIs and privatization. The analysis presented in the preceding section suggests that the actual form of ownership is less important than the university's or college's academic mission. In addition, the unique relationship of even small HEIs to global academic norms limits the impact that changes in ownership relations will have on academic governance. These findings are particularly important for the Arab world, which recently has been near or at the forefront of movements to restructure the higher education system.

The reasons for this push to create a private sector of universities and colleges vary from country to country. In some nations, the demographic boom combined with improved secondary school attainment and general commitments to provide higher education seats for high school graduates has threatened to swamp existing public universities. While students from poorer families have less ability to attend tuition-driven educational institutions, middle-class families are increasingly turning to the private sector, which often promises smaller class sizes, instruction in English, and better facilities. This development has the added advantage of reducing financial pressure on countries that often face extreme budgetary pressures. Even the GCC countries are facing these difficulties in an era of low oil prices.

In addition to the problem of accommodating new generations of students, the problematic economic performance of most Arab countries since 2011 has led critics to focus on problems within Arab universities. Whether fairly or not, the argument is often made that public HEIs in the Middle East fail to promote creative thinking and rigorous inquiry (UNDP 2003). Thus, it is felt that private universities could more readily break with backward academic practices that frustrate the creation of knowledge-based economies led by private entrepreneurs.

While these tendencies are not unique to the Arab world, there is one feature of this region's reform movement that has implications for the governance of these new institutions. This is the tendency to import curricular models with administrators from outside the region. Thus, with a few exceptions, the movement of higher education reform is a top-down process that is either imposed on existing faculty or implemented by the importation of new academics who are unfamiliar with the region. Such a process challenges faculty governance. Conflicts between administrators and faculty are not uncommon in most universities and colleges, but in this case, higher education leaders can impose their will on a staff whose fallback position (the next-best alternative source of employment) is not attractive. This problem could be exacerbated by authoritarian political systems that tend to suppress dissent in any event.

This would suggest that the motivation for privatization is more important to the viability of an academic institution than the fact of privatization itself. If the goal of the new owners, or the nonprofit board of trustees acting on behalf of new owners, is to create a prestigious private institution that upholds global academic standards, then the pressure to conform to international expectations will be considerable. If the goal of the owner is to establish a profitable business that can pay off the investments of the owner in a short period of time, then it will be more difficult for regulatory authorities to maintain academic quality and more difficult for faculty teaching in this institution to have an effective voice.

As the examples of Qatar University and the University of the United Arab Emirates demonstrate, the reform of public universities in the Arab world is a complex process. Here reformers must respond more directly to well-established opponents of reform who can resist or at least challenge efforts to remake higher education practices. These pressures might come from parents unhappy with a change of standards, or from government officials whose own decision-making power over HEIs has been weakened. In authoritarian societies that discourage public dialogue and protest, the faculty might have little role to play. Previously practiced methods of collaborative day-to-day governance are replaced by new methods that can divide faculty and erode the morale of professors. This is especially true if new administrators are imported into the country to establish new academic standards.

Conclusion

The pressures exerted on faculty by higher education reform and privatization in the Arab world are paradoxical. On the one hand, this chapter's analysis implies that the participation of faculty in the running of universities and colleges will remain important whether or not the institution is public or private. On the other hand, the drive to create educational establishments in the image of Western institutions can erode local autonomy and weaken the authority of local academics.

The analysis of the GCC finds support for both conclusions, but it should be noted that the Arabian Peninsula is a very idiosyncratic place. In terms of academic institutions, these oddities include national universities that largely exclude expatriate students and include the presence of a considerable expatriate academic staff with fewer rights and protections than one would find in most other parts of the world. The result is that the faculty can be forced to respond to rapid changes in policy and often find that the contracts they sign do not provide protection from arbitrary dismissal. With respect to the new educational establishments, these private universities and colleges have a more diverse student body, but members of the faculty also have few formal rights. A further result of this split between nationals and expatriates is a cultural and sometimes linguistic gulf between teachers, students, and the general national populations of the region.

Despite this unusual setting, my own assessment is that the global nature of the higher education enterprises tends to promote over time collaborative forms of academic governance throughout the world rather than impede them. Academics must have substantial autonomy within the classroom if teaching is to be effective, and research also requires that academics have the ability to explore topics of their choosing. Research publication must then be evaluated by experts outside the control of the administrative staff. These autonomous tasks are further buttressed by international regulatory agency officials who emphasize the importance of collaborative governance and who are guided by shared academic norms learned by all faculty members who have received advanced graduate training. Thus, the maintenance and strengthening of these forms of academic management are most likely to be found in institutions that are located in countries that emphasize the importance of international accreditation and link the establishment of robust HEIs to projects that promote economic reform.

This does not mean that all education reform in the Arab world has promoted collaborative governance. There is clear evidence that certain types of for-profit HEIs do not promote education quality and do not encourage the participation of faculty in the management of their workplace. Nevertheless, the pressure to create a more modern university sector that is integrated with the rest of the world is strong in the Arab world. The privatization process, if pursued in the context of strong international regulatory supervision sponsored by governmental authority, can contribute to the creation of a stronger and more creative higher education sector.

References

Badry, Fatima, and Willoughby, John (2015). *Higher education revolutions in the gulf.* London: Routledge.

Ghabra, S. (2010). Student centered education and American style universities in the Arab world. *Higher education and the Middle East: Empowering underserved and vulnerable populations* (pp. 21–26). Washington, DC: Middle East Institute.

Moini, J. S., Bikson, T. K., Neu, C. R., and DeSisto, L. (2009). *The Reform of Qatar University.* Santa Monica: Rand Corporation.

UNDP (2003). *Arab human development report 2003: Building a knowledge society.* New York: UNDP.

Williamson, Oliver (1996). *The mechanisms of governance.* Oxford: Oxford University Press.

John Willoughby is Professor of Economics at American University in Washington, D.C. He is the co-author of the book *Higher Education Revolutions in the Gulf* (2015). He has also published scholarly articles on gender relations and migration with respect to the Arabian Peninsula. He has taught as a Visiting Professor at the American University in Cairo, the American University of Sharjah, and Zayed University.

The Role of Governance in Promoting the Presence of Women in Higher Education Institutions in the Arab World

Madonna Salameh-Ayanian and Diala Kozaily

Governance in the Arab World

Governance is the art of leading an entity according to the principles of sustainability in order to reach its objective. It is the context in which a body ensures an accountable, fair, and transparent relationship with its stakeholders. The Arab world only recently became aware of the significance of governance and its impact on the development of their nations. Today, systems are criticized, practices are questioned, and scandals resonate, making the importance of preserving one's credibility even greater. With globalization, changes in economic models, the internationalization of commerce, and the digital invasion of our daily lives, governance appears to be the primary route to success. It is thus a mandatory weapon for survival in the face of an extremely challenging environment and for ensuring a place in this "global village." As governance stems from words associated with equality, transparency, good

M. Salameh-Ayanian (✉) · D. Kozaily
Holy Spirit University of Kaslik (USEK), Jounieh, Lebanon
e-mail: madonnasalameh@usek.edu.lb; diala.y.kozaily@net.usek.edu.lb

© The Author(s) 2018
G. Azzi (ed.), *Higher Education Governance in the Arab World*,
DOI 10.1007/978-3-319-52060-5_8

147

practice, development, and empowerment, one cannot but address the harsh reality faced by those who would implement governance principles in the Arab world, especially when it comes to gender disparity. Governance in the Arab world is facing major problems, mainly from the local culture, which is characterized by corruption. Although the Arab world are all connected in various ways—by language, geographical proximity, and religion, not to mention certain traditions and social expectations—there is great divergence in the political, social, and economic factors that shape them. These differences are mostly related to their cultural heritage as well as the developmental stage that each country is experiencing. It is, however, clearly apparent that women play only minimal roles in these countries, because the region is far from instituting practices in support of gender equity. Its authoritarian regimes, outdated education systems, security threats, and overall unemployment rates position the region at the lower end of the spectrum with regard to having a fair governance system in place. It is true that the situation could be better; nevertheless, it is important to state that the Arab world is progressing toward better governance practices in all fields, especially after the Arab Spring. Considered by many as an uprising by the region itself, the Arab Spring aimed initially to break down authoritarian resilience, and it created hope for the empowerment of women (Aarts et al. 2012). Since empowering women resonates the most through education, the next part of this chapter considers governance in the Arab educational sector.

Governance and the Education Sector

As the world gradually develops new governance techniques and practices, the Arab world does as well—but according to its own rhythm. If governance reform is taking place, it is because it is being implemented in different and varied sectors, one of which is education. More precisely, higher education institutions (HEIs) are raising awareness and conceptualizing policies to implement effective governance strategies; these changes are influencing other sectors, encouraging them to venture into similar areas. HEIs are investing in applying transparency and accountability reforms, and adopting international standards, in order to gain a place within the international higher education community and to feed the market with the appropriate human capital. Education is considered a way to build social cohesion, break wrongdoing, and ensure innovation and continuous advancement. Through education, communities are built and societies are shaped. Playing a major role in forging the personality of its members, education transmits values and beliefs and impacts personalities and attitudes while stimulating students' intellect. When channeled in the right direction, education has the ability to help individuals achieve their highest potential to the benefit of society, reducing poverty and capitalizing on the technological improvements and globalization that are further increasing opportunities for advancement. To achieve this ultimate goal, HEIs have created official quality assurance offices that aim to create value throughout their processes while encouraging the development of a learning culture. They are now modifying program structures in order to better adapt to market needs and international standards. The higher education industry is becoming more diverse and experiencing rapid changes at all levels; the promotion of governance requires changes to several aspects of an institution, including putting in place systems to track and avoid corruption and wrongdoing while promoting equality and fair practice. Collective participation—by involving various stakeholders in management processes and establishing a board of trustees or governance board—and the design of the curricula offered are necessary elements in changing an organization's culture so that it encompasses governance principles that are geared toward sustainable development and growth. Having a quality matrix across all institutional aspects and departments as well as transparency and accountability measures will also foster integrity in managing and coping with change while monitoring performance. However, total reform cannot occur unless women's role within these institutions is further strengthened and supported. The higher education industry has a high rate of women employees and instructors; however, the number of women in top management positions in these institutions is extremely low, if not zero.

The reform in HEIs will provide multiple benefits that will impact the society at large; these benefits will expand beyond the scope of the universities to encompass the society, the economy, and the international position and reputation of the individuals of a nation:

1. HEIs are the primary source of knowledge; they play a fundamental role in defining the future paths of individuals and are a main pillar in shaping their personalities; improvements in the system and the culture in place will have direct repercussions for individuals who spend a substantial part of their lives within these institutions. An effective system will lead to individuals being better able to internalize ethical principles in addition to their quality technical skills and expertise. Raised differently, these university students will tackle the world differently—raising the bar for equal and ethical practices in every aspect of their lives.

2. Improvements in the quality of education will create better candidates for local and international corporations located in the Arab world. Quality people promote the societies and the countries they represent; they constitute a source of increased innovation for the development of new business ventures and entrepreneurial activities across key sectors. Such activities have a direct impact on the development of a nation's economy and its international appeal while promoting a spirit of continuous research and a quest for excellence—drivers of a nation's development and competitiveness.

3. Arab universities will be better placed to compete at the global level by setting clear governance principles, by obtaining international accreditation, and by advancing in the rankings. In order to survive and to ensure a competitive position in the market, they must provide quality education that is recognized by international bodies and other countries. With the increased mobility of individuals, ensuring that their programs are recognized in the majority of key markets will give them a competitive advantage in attracting the right candidates.

4. Reform in HEIs will allow the Arab world to attract foreign players, educators, and students and facilitate easier incorporation of Arab students into foreign universities. The Arab world continues to have

several untapped areas of opportunity that are of interest to foreign countries, and attracting students, educators, and business owners who can reap the benefits and capitalize on such areas is undoubtedly possible; this would constitute a safer ground for investors who might be interested in this field, as well as enable the development of joint initiatives ranging from professor and student exchanges to dual diplomas and joint ventures.

When speaking about reform, equal employment opportunities and empowerment of women are key elements. The place of women in the higher education industry is clearly affected by the local and regional culture; for that reason, it is important to understand the position of women in the Arab world.

The Place of Women in the MENA Region

When it comes to the place of women in the Middle East and North Africa (MENA) region, it is important to mention that the participation of men and women in public, corporate, and social life differs among the countries and falls more in favor of men. Women constitute more than half of the population of the Arab world; however, they are not regarded as capable human beings. In some countries they are not permitted to drive, to vote, to work in certain fields, and so on. Arab women are still fighting to gain their basic rights.

Several factors prohibit women from playing an active strategic or decisional role in society; these include the culture, gender stereotypes, and motherhood. Arab literature traditionally presents women as inferior creatures, and in some cases they start to act as such; they tend to behave according to society's expectations, and therefore their perception of their own ability to perform is negatively affected and they have low self-esteem. Encouraged to marry at an early age, women handle all domestic obligations while men, labeled as the "head of the family," have to secure an income and protect the family. This label gives men the authority to dictate to women their role inside and outside the household. From a cultural and traditional point of view, the socialization of the roles of men and women is very strong; this sociocultural reality explains the gender inequalities in the workplace. Women are permitted to perform work activities outside the home only when they can first and foremost fulfill their obligations at home. This is one explanation for women's lack of representation in corporate board seats of governmental bodies—an indicator of the vast gender gap that exists in the majority of the countries. It appears that women tend to stagnate at the middle point within organizations, where an invisible barrier seems to exist to prohibit them from advancing further. As a matter of fact, historically men have held and still do hold top decisional seats, making it difficult to imagine women holding similar positions; the absence of proven successful female participation and leadership makes it even harder to envision a woman succeeding in doing so. To go further, additional barriers exist, as women are not allowed to work in certain industries that are considered dangerous; they are also—in the case of Saudi Arabia, the UAE, and Oman—prohibited from working night shifts unless they are employed in medicine or certain other fields (Kelly 2009).

Several laws based on religion have an unfavorable impact on women's ability to contribute to society. According to Metcalfe et al. (2011), Islam and sharia law, as well as cultural practices and *urf* (custom), emphasize the need to protect women and to create a morally adequate working environment. Furthermore, the slow rate of economic growth has further impacted negatively the place of women. If the rate of male unemployment increases, the government will put less emphasis on encouraging females to enter the workplace. According to the Organisation for Economic Co-operation and Development (OECD) (2014), women are more affected by unemployment, are the first to lose their jobs, and have to wait longer to find new ones. As a matter of fact, the Middle East scores the lowest worldwide in terms of women's active participation; however, when it comes to education of females, the rate is rapidly increasing. Women make up 6% of the parliament in Kuwait and 3% in Lebanon, while in Algeria, women constitute 30% of congress, exceeding the global average of 21.8%, according to data from the Inter-Parliamentary Union (IPU), (2014). It is however noteworthy, that despite occupying such positions, it is noticeable that women fail to generate the necessary impact and remain among the weakest performers in terms of effective contributors for growth at the national level. Additionally, no women have yet managed to become president of any of the Arab world.

Nevertheless, the situation is changing. Women are raising their voices, and success stories are paving the way for others to dare to take up the challenge and to question and revolt against common prejudices. Several initiatives have been taken to increase the active role of women; these include quotas requiring that a certain number of leadership seats be filled by women. Countries have now developed national strategies that aim to foster gender equality while empowering women and fighting discriminatory practices. Table 1 highlights a few of the endeavors undertaken in this regard.

It is undeniable that women view the world differently from men; they have the ability to bring new insights and consider things from different perspectives, thus stimulating innovation. Moreover, it is believed that the presence of women in strategic corporate positions is associated with positive financial returns. Women continue to invest in their education, obtaining higher diplomas than their male counterparts; with education, capacity building, leadership training, and recognition

Table 1 National gender equality strategies

Country	Name of strategy
Bahrain	The National Plan for the advancement of Bahraini women (2013–2022)
Egypt	Egyptian council for women (NCW) Strategy for Gender Equality
Jordan	National Strategy for women in Jordan (2012–2015)
Lebanon	National Strategy for women in Lebanon (2011–2021); and National Action Plan (2013–2016)
Morocco	L'Agenda gouvernemental pour l'égalité 2011–2015
Palestinian Authority	Cross-Sectorial National Gender Strategy 2011–2013
Tunisia	Stratégie de la lutte contre la violence à l'égard des femmes au sein de la famille et de la société
Yemen	National Strategy for women's development (2006–2015)
UAE	National Strategy for women's advancement (2002–2014)

Source: OECD Survey on National Gender Frameworks, Gender Public Policies and Leadership (updated in 2014)

of the dual role that women need to fulfill within their household, women will be able to generate further impact. Jalbout (2015) states that if women worked in the same numbers as men, the GDP of every Arab state would increase. In the United Arab Emirates (UAE), an equal number of women and men working would raise the country's GDP by 12%; in Egypt, the same achievement would raise GDP by 34%. For nations to flourish, affirmative action to support women's role in society is key, as governance principles consider the presence and active participation of women as well as their inclusion among board members and in high-level positions in government and social initiatives.

The Evolution

Although the situation of women in the Arab world is difficult, women have achieved significant results through continual perseverance, dedication, and self-development. The role of women has become a central focus for international programs and conferences; many actions have been taken to increase their presence in society in general and in governance management in particular. Activities such as the International Women's Year and the Decade for Women have been announced in order to improve women's status in the Arab world and to enable them to reflect upon their current situation while emphasizing areas for improvement. Tools, funds, coaching, and mentoring programs are being proposed, supported by national and international organizations such as the World Bank, the United Nations (UN), and the UN Educational, Scientific and Cultural Organization (UNESCO), as well as local and regional organizations, whether public, private, for-profit or non-governmental organizations (NGOs), with the aim of providing tools and platforms for their development. Increased enrollment of women in universities, socioeconomic changes, and modernization and globalization processes together facilitated the participation of Arab women in the labor market and created additional opportunities for women to have an active role in society; the higher education industry was also touched by these changes.

Nevertheless, it is undeniable that a woman's self-image affects her decisions. According to the 2016 publication of Internet World Stats, 57.4% of people in the Middle East use the Internet, and the Middle East had the second-highest increase in Internet usage between 2000 and 2016 worldwide after Africa, with a rate of growth of 4,207.4%. Stories from both the East and the West now make their way to each and every individual. Women now see, hear, and view other women succeeding and making changes, and thus they further dare to take up the challenge and venture into new areas. All these changes have generated opportunities for women to participate in the decision-making processes across several institutions. Here we can mention that numerous women have proven themselves capable of achieving good results when given power. As a matter of fact, more than a few Arab women are ranked among the most successful and powerful women in the world. Some of the names that come to mind include Mona Bawarchi, CEO of Gezairi Transport s.a.l., a well-known transportation company in the Arab world, who was mentioned in an article about successful women in the September 2016 issue of *Le Commerce du Levant*. Mona Bawarchi is also a member of the board of trustees of a number of colleges and HEIs in the Arab world. Another woman who can be mentioned for her direct contribution to governance in HEIs is Her Highness Sheikha Moza bint Nasser. Her Highness is the chairperson of the Qatar Foundation for Education and is part of other governmental and non-governmental organizations, and she has been nominated by UNESCO as a special correspondent for basic and higher education in recognition of her exceptional role in promoting education in Qatar. She demonstrated her support for Iraq by creating a higher education fund for the country as a personal initiative. Moreover, Dr. Amal Almalki, described as "an inspirational author and professor" by Kassis (2015), is a real advocate for liberal and powerful Arab women through her academic career—teaching and writing—and public speaking. Furthermore, the Queen of Jordan, Her Majesty Rania Al-Yassin or al-Abdallah Rania, is a liberal female voice from within the heart of the Arab world, an activist for reform in education, and a strong defender of Arab women's rights. All these names and many others are honorable examples that show the constructive influence of Arab women in their countries and serve as exceptional role models for Arab women to follow.

Despite all the obstacles women face, one major characteristic defines them today: Women are determined to work hard in order to prove their real worth and have equal rights to men. Women managers have several opportunities for growth. In general, their special psychological qualities—such as cooperation; good communication and negotiation; and the ability to solve problems, be rationally and emotionally balanced, and be highly ethical—make them good candidates for achieving results in governing HEIs. Significant improvements to women's roles in HEIs cannot be achieved if society does not take responsibility for providing a central role for women as scholars, decision-makers, policymakers, contributors, and organizers.

On the one hand, governance in HEIs in the Arab world is setting a course for change and development. On the other hand, women inside and outside those institutions are proving themselves capable of achieving good results and influencing the education sector. Hence, what role will women play in governance reform in HEIs in the Arab world?

Women in Higher Education Institutions

Higher education is the source that provides society with qualified and professional experts for all industries. It is thus the fountain of knowledge and the driver of innovation through scientific research and experiments. The presence of women within such institutions is of strategic importance for society at large; women educators and leaders within this field constitute role models for others to follow, as they are the educators of the leaders of tomorrow.

According to a World Economic Forum report by Schwab and Sala-i-Martin (2015), women's empowerment revolves around four dimensions: participation in economic life, level of education, health and survival, and political empowerment. The majority of the Arab world obtain low scores in these areas, especially those related to levels of economic and political participation by women. Education performs better.

As a matter of fact, women are seen to perform best in industries in which their gender qualities are seen to be associated with the activities within that industry. These include education, health, and care. The education sector is regarded by the majority of the population as an honorable, superior domain, a place where it is suitable for women to be present—in brief, an environment that does not challenge social and religious beliefs. Qatar and the UAE have the highest rate of female-to-male enrollment in HEIs worldwide; however, there is an unequal distribution across disciplines. Fields such as engineering, construction, mathematics, and manufacturing are still dominated by male students, while teaching, health and welfare, and social sciences are favored by women. Globally, the number of female students rose sixfold, from 10.8 to 77.4 million, between 1970 and 2008 (UNESCO 2010). Nevertheless, the number of women in administrative positions decreases as they advance on the hierarchical ladder. In the USA, women held only 27% of presidencies across all HEIs as of 2011 (Heather 2016); it was also noted that these women presidents are less likely to be married, less likely to have children, and more likely to have chosen a career over family.

According to Abu-Orabi (2013), only 13 public and private universities had been established in the Arab world as of 1953; however, by 2006 there were 286 universities in the Arab world, of which 153 were governmental and 133 were private. By 2012 the number had risen to more than 500 universities, with around nine million students and 250,000 faculty members. Although enrollment predominates in public universities, the ratio of private versus public university enrollment is considered high in this region, totaling 40% in comparison to 20% in the USA, while the number of researchers per million inhabitants is 450 in the Arab world compared to 5,000 per million inhabitants in developed countries. Based on data from a UNESCO (2010) report on governments' investments in education, Table 2 provides a comparative analysis of the

Table 2 Total public expenditure on education as a percentage of GDP (%)

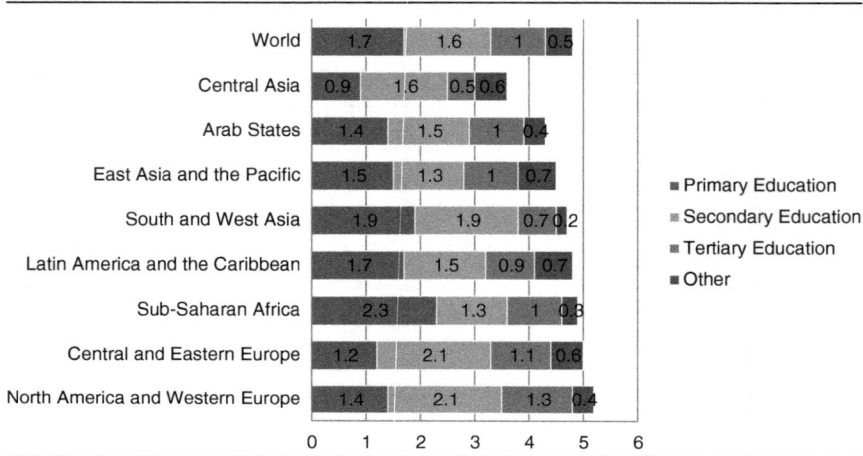

Source: Public expenditure on education: UNESCO institute for statistics database of statistical table 15; GDP: World Bank
Notes: "Other" includes expenditure for pre-primary education and unallocated expenditure. World and regional averages are calculated based on 145 countries with available data over the period 2007–2009, representing 83% of the world total GDP in PPP$
Number of countries covered by region: North Africa and Western Europe (24/29), Central and Eastern Europe (16/21), Sub-Saharan Africa (35/45), Latin America and the Caribbean (25/42), South and West Asia (7/9), East Asia and the Pacific (17/34), Arab States (14/20), and Central Asia (7/9)

differences between regions; we can note the percentage of GDP for education as of 2009.

Although the above representation includes only primary, secondary, and tertiary education, the figures show that the region is at the low end of the spectrum, indicating that higher education expenditure by governments is certainly lagging behind the global average, despite the efforts being taken in this regard.

However, it is worth recognizing the rise in the number of universities in the region; Table 3 provides an understanding of the repartition by higher educational type per country for 2011 as communicated by the

Table 3 Key numbers per country—type and number of universities, number of students and faculty staff in 2003 and 2011

Country	2003 Gov.	2003 Private	2003 Total	2011 Gov.	2011 Private	2011 Total	Number of students	Number of faculty staff
Tunisia	8	14	22	13	19	32	360000	21210
Iraq	14	-	14	25	8	33	397784	31990
Bahrain	2	-	2	2	8	10	35848	3100
Yemen	7	8	15	8	13	21	300000	10000
UAE	2	5	7	2	19	21	59333	1961
Morocco	13	1	14	14	4	18	419885	12085
Sudan	27	1	28	28	7	35	500000	9700
Lebanon	1	18	19	1	19	20	205000	12700
Oman	1	1	2	1	7	8	80000	4100
Kuwait	1	2	3	1	4	5	34560	1705
Saudi Arabia	8	-	8	23	8	31	667000	21320
Syria	5	-	5	5	10	15	282484	9500
Egypt	13	6	19	20	15	35	2800000	67000
Palestine	2	9	11	2	13	15	196625	5900
Jordan	8	10	18	11	18	29	336000	8898
Libya	14	-	14	9	2	11	264000	9000
Somalia	1	2	3	3	11	14	4147	195
Comoros	-	-	-	1	-	1		-
Mauritania	1	-	1	1	-	1	25000	1175
Djibouti	1	-	1	1	-	1	15000	580
Qatar	1	-	1	1	6	7	15500	1100
Algeria	26	-	26	34	2	36	1149899	19500
Total	156	77	233	206	193	399	8148065	252619

Source: Arab Society of Faculties of Business, Economics and Political Sciences as delivered in the presentation of Abu-Orabi (2013) in the conference.

Arab Society of Faculties of Business, Economics and Political Sciences, as presented by Abu Orabi (2013).

Based on the number mentioned above, HEIs are witnessing a noticeable increase, yet the growth rate differs from one country to another. The increase in number requires the availability of qualified members to serve the needs of and deliver quality education, providing further opportunities for women to venture into this domain and grow. However, it must be stated that there has been a decrease in the level of representation of women in middle management and senior management positions on governing boards and councils; the number of top management positions held by women remains in single figures across the majority of these institutions, while the same situation exists on departmental and faculty committees. There are some notable differences between countries, however. With regard to higher education in Saudi Arabia, according to a report by the Ministry of Higher Education in Saudi Arabia, more than 300 HEIs existed in 2010, with 56% of students in the country being women, and a special university for women—Princess Noura bint Abdul Rahman University for Women—was established with the aim of becoming the world's largest center of higher education for women worldwide. Dr. Khawla Al-Kurai, chief cancer researcher at King Faisal Research Center, received her King Abdulaziz first class order in recognition of her distinguished work in medicine and her international awards in the field. Professors Samira Ibrahim Islam, Ghada Al Mutairi, Hayat Hindi, Howaida Obaid al-Qethamy, and Soraya Al Turki are also notable examples of Saudi women who have made significant contributions in the academic and scientific research fields. In addition, Mrs. Noura El Fayez is the first woman to hold the position of vice minister of education for women's affairs. However, the situation in this country has received strong criticism, in particular with regard to the extent to which the development of initiatives to support women while separating them from their male counterparts could really be considered governance practices.

An overview of women's representation on governance boards is essential to help us further understand the present situation.

In Lebanon, a few women have managed to overcome the status quo and secure seats on the governing bodies of HEIs. Boards of directors have been established at several key institutions and women are filling some seats. According to their official website, the composition of the boards of the top six universities in Lebanon is as follows:

- Lebanese American University (LAU)—six women out of 28 board members;
- Holy Spirit University of Kaslik (USEK)—one woman out of 18 board members;
- American University of Beirut (AUB)—six women out of 40 members of the board of trustees, and four women out of 27 Emeriti board members;
- Notre Dame University (NDU)—three women out of 24 board members;
- Balamand University—one woman out of 33 board members;
- Saint Joseph University (USJ)—three women out of 29 members of the strategic board.

Below are figures pertaining to some other universities in the region:

- In Egypt, the American University of Cairo (AUC) has eight women out of 33 board members, as well as three women out of 20 advisory trustees.
- In the United Arab Emirates, the American University of Dubai (AUD) has no women on its governing board, which comprises six men, while the American University of Sharjah has two women out of 17 board members.
- In Saudi Arabia, King Abdullah University of Science and Technology has one woman out of ten local board members and three women out of 14 foreign board members, while King Fahd University of Petroleum and Minerals has no women on its board.
- In Nigeria, the Nigeria Higher Education Foundation (NHEF) includes two women out of six board members.

- In Jordan, the Jordan University of Science and Technology has one woman out of 13 board members, while the German Jordanian University has three women out of 13 board members.
- In Morocco, the ESCA Ecole de Management has eight women out of 30 board members.
- In Qatar, the Qatar University has no women among its 11 board members.

It is worth mentioning that several universities in this region do not yet have governing boards; however, in their quest for international accreditation, they now recognize the necessity of establishing a diverse board of directors that includes stakeholders from various disciplines and provides enriching insights while broadening horizons and increasing opportunities.

Careers in Higher Education

These encouraging and increasing figures indicate an opportunity for women instructors, who are becoming more and more present within HEIs, to advance. The career paths of individuals within HEIs usually follow a predefined pattern that links the level of study or degree obtained, research work, and publications, as well as seniority and experience, to advancement on the hierarchical ladder. Classifications include instructor, lecturer, assistant professor, associate professor, professor, and distinguished professor, while the positions can range from instructor, head of department, and associate dean to dean, and from there to board member, deputy president, provost, or president. However, the factors that can interrupt such advancement or halt it might include a variety of internal factors related to the individual him or herself, or external factors related to the institution or to the general macro environment within which the individual is operating.

Women in particular find their advancement opportunities and decisions determined by a variety of factors, which can be summed up as follows:

- **Internal personal factors** include the intrinsic elements that are unique to each and every person and are shaped by the way a woman was raised, her present situation in the household, and her personal business experience. These factors could be related to:

  - **Financial capacity and budget** that is to be allocated for further educational advancement; higher education is costly, aside from the public universities. In some cases, the cost of Master's or postgraduate studies is relatively high in private institutions and can deter talented individuals from seeking higher degrees.
  - **Priority in relation to work–life balance,** where individuals might personally avoid advancing in the hierarchy in order to maintain a certain level of stability; as mentioned earlier, household obligations are mostly the responsibility of women, and by committing to more demanding jobs, their presence at home is affected. This can cause women to avoid promotions in some circumstances.
  - **Maternity,** which can cause a partial or complete interruption in a woman's career; maternity leads to absenteeism, a factor that is not regarded positively by corporate owners. Recruitment decisions are sometimes biased in favor of men based on the assumption that women's state of mind and priorities will change after they have a child.
  - **Fear of the unknown and self-image** is related to the internalized view that women have about themselves, in addition to psychological factors that can lead to an individual questioning their capacity to handle, manage, and succeed within such positions. Several women have incorporated the general statements shared about them in this regard, and consider themselves not up to the challenge when it comes to increased responsibility at work.
  - **Support of one's family and partner** is also a key driver in motivating women to accept new challenges at work. In this part of the world, the family plays a major role in the life of an individual; their support or lack of it dictates the individual's path. When women have family support in raising their

children and handling household obligations, they feel more confident and reassured about the well-being of their household and thus invest more time in their career. In the absence of such support, women are more likely to pass up numerous opportunities.

- **Access:** The ease of access to certain degrees, such as doctoral and post-doctoral programs, which might require mobility or travel, is an important factor; this is not appealing for women, especially when they are married and have children.

• **External factors** are the ones that the individual does not have direct control over; these appear as a culmination of cultural and societal practices and norms that impact the situation of women. They include:

  - **Gender stereotypes:** The general perceptions and beliefs that women are weak, incapable, and highly emotional; accordingly, it becomes difficult to appoint or even accept women managers.
  - **Proven record:** Top management positions are mostly filled by men, and they tend to promote individuals who look like them; lack of knowledge about the contributions that women could make in such positions raises barriers to their appointment.
  - **Networking and mobility:** Top management positions often require that a dynamic and interactive network is maintained at both the local and the international level. This may not be possible for a woman with a family to care for. In some cultures, it is not acceptable for a woman to be part of certain networks or even to travel to some countries without a male family member to accompany her and grant her access.
  - **National and organizational cultures** that include visible discriminatory rules and regulations in addition to biased human resource (HR) management policies and promotional plans. The national culture is a cumulative experience of what our ancestors have lived and shared; to change the culture takes time and might sometimes require strong manifestations to turn things upside down and to effect real change.

Improvements are certainly happening; however, nations and organizations still need to go through several phases before achieving total equality. At the corporate level, organizational culture is a direct reflection of the beliefs of a firm's founders. Through internal rules and regulations as reflected in HR policies and practices, equality is possible. Support from top management is the main driver in installing a more balanced team at the very top of an organization.

- **Lack of proper legislation:** Rules and regulations exist to preserve the rights of individuals; legislation can impose certain conditions that can further encourage the active participation of women in society. Quotas, for instance, are a method that several European countries have successfully adopted, along with changes in legislation to further preserve the rights of women while taking into consideration the duality of their roles.

- **Technological advancements** are creating opportunities and providing access to several educational programs around the world; with distance learning, video conferences, and online teaching and learning methods, boundaries are brought closer and access to education becomes easier.

The above-mentioned factors are elements of what is called the glass ceiling phenomenon: an invisible barrier that prohibits equally qualified individuals from advancing. In this case, the glass ceiling prevents women from moving from middle management positions into upper managerial roles. This problem needs to be resolved in order for real governance to be put in place. To overcome the situation, several initiatives are needed:

- Access to education via grants and funds: National and organizational budgets should be designated to support and encourage women to develop their knowledge and present them with further opportunities to improve their skills.
- Review of legislation to include quotas and practical national strategies to support women's participation in all fields.

- Reconsideration and reformulation of the HR policies and practices in place, while considering the work–life balance component by putting in place facilities and services to help parents pursue their careers. These include adopting new HR concepts such as flextime, a compressed work week, job sharing, and working from home. In addition, gender equality policies, such as equal employment opportunities, should be established, and career advancement and promotion should be considered from the beginning of the recruitment process.
- Training and development in areas related to leadership and managerial skills; such opportunities would help women further develop themselves and exchange their experiences of learning curves and best practices while reflecting on their roles and capabilities in order to build synergies between the roles they have to assume and their role as women.
- A change in the culture, which starts with an endorsement of the role of women and the importance of their contribution to the growth of each institution. Women have to contribute significantly to the development of HEIs; they too need to be in higher administrative positions in order to influence policy- and decision-making. Systems and structures should be modernized to help shape a better and more stable society while providing the opportunity to access such positions.

Governance: The Way Forward

In the face of the political instability that characterizes the Arab world, as well as the vast amount of talent that is wasted due to exclusionary structures and salary discrepancies, it is undeniable that social injustice is limiting the opportunities for women—the source of life of all human beings—to further prove themselves. In order to achieve, advance, and succeed, women need first and foremost to understand the governing system that is in place, as well as the legislation that constitutes guiding references for all actions. Moreover, they need to participate more actively in committees and structures so that they can further comprehend the rationale that shapes these institutions and leads to the implementation of certain processes and practices. A woman should understand that it is necessary for her to capitalize on her strengths by actively engaging in activities in which she can prove herself capable while promoting her ideas. This will certainly impact perceptions; although this may happen at a slow rate, it will eventually lead to further acceptance and belief in the capacity of women to perform and to contribute to the development of the institution in which they are present. By becoming agents of change, women can overcome stereotypes and generate further opportunities. Women can certainly bring an enriched experience to the table; as a matter of fact, diversity management concepts stress the importance and positive contribution of a diverse workforce to the success of a company.

Today it has become incontestable that women are capable; the challenge lies in establishing the needed infrastructure and ensuring fair practice in both public and private systems. Complete reform is needed across all sectors—and governance is the solution. If the educators of the leaders of tomorrow do not have the opportunity to lead, then the entire educational system needs to be revised. Last but not least, overcoming these barriers requires a change in the way both men and women are raised, starting in the household and continuing throughout the educational journey. The responsibility lies first and foremost with women themselves, who should raise the leaders of tomorrow based on principles of equality starting from a very early age at home, in the way they deal with and nurture their sons and daughters. Additionally, joining hands with other women and providing them with encouragement and support would help to create a solid community.

As a concluding remark, the higher education industry worldwide is embracing governance principles and thus setting a high bar for both newcomers and existing players. A new era has undoubtedly begun, and governance is the way forward, with the place of women as a focal point. Now that women's issues are making the news, and putting women in the spotlight, how will they impact the course of history in a world that is witnessing increased existential challenges?

References

Aarts, P., Dijke, P. V., Kolman, I., Statema, J., and Dahhan, G. (2012). From resilience to revolt: Making sense of the Arab spring.

Heather, J. (2016). *Pipelines, pathways, and institutional leadership: An update on the status of women in higher education.* Washington, DC: American Council on Education.

Jalbout, M. (2015). "Unlocking the potential of educated Arab women", Brookings Institute. Retrieved from http://www.brookings.edu/blogs/educa tion-plus-development/posts/2015/03/12-unlocking-potential-educatio narab-women-jalbout.

Kelly, S. (2009). Recent gains and new opportunities for women's rights in the Gulf Arab states, in *Women's Rights in the Middle East and North Africa: Gulf Edition*, 1–8. Washington, DC: Freedom House.

LINKING MED GULF's Kick-off Meeting was held at the University of Barcelona on January 21, 2013—Sultan Abu Orabi—Scientific research and Arab education in the Arab world.

Metcalfe, B. D., Murfin, T., Metcalfe, B. D., and Mimouni, F. (2011). Leadership, social development and political economy in the Middle East: An introduction. *Leadership Development in the Middle East*, 1–60. Edward Elgar Publishing.

Morley, L. (2013). *Women and higher education leadership: Absences and aspirations: Stimulus paper* for the Leadership Foundation for Higher Education. London: LFHE.

OECD /CWTAR (2014). *Women in public life: Gender, law and policy in the Middle East and North Africa.* OECD publishing, Paris. Retrieved from: http://dx.doi.org/10.1787/9789264224636-en.

Schwab, K., and Sala-i-Martin, X. (2015). World Economic Forum's Global Competitiveness Report, 2014–2015. *Retrieved from:* http://reports. weforum.org/global-competitiveness-report-2014–2015/. *Switzerland: World Economic Forum.*

UNESCO Institute of Statistics (2010). *Global education digest (2010). Comparing education statistics across the world (A Special Focus on Gender).* Paris: UNESCO.

Inter-Parliamentary Union (2014). Women in parliaments by regions. Geneva, Switzerland, http://www.ipu.org/wmn-e/world.htm, *15*, 2014. Accessed on December 17, 2016.

Web references

American University of Beirut (2016). http://www.aub.edu.lb/main/about/Pages/bot.aspx. Accessed on November 10, 2016.
American University of Sharjah (2016).
https://www.aus.edu/info/200131/board_of_trustees. Accessed on November 10, 2016.
American University in Dubai (2016). http://www.aud.edu/about_aud/en/page/1134/governing-board. Accessed on November 10, 2016.
ESCA Ecole de Management (2016).
http://www.esca.ma/esca/gouvernance. Accessed on November 10, 2016.
Holy Spirit University of Kaslik (2016).
http://www.usek.edu.lb/en/about-usek/board-of-trustees. Accessed on November 10, 2016.
Internet World Stats, Usage and Population statistics (2016). http://www.internetworldstats.com/stats.htm. Accessed on November 10, 2016.
Jordan University of Science and Technology (2016). http://www.just.edu.jo/aboutjust/Presidency/Pages/BoardOfTrustees.aspx. Accessed on November 10, 2016.
Kassis, J. (2015). http://executive-women.com/2015/07/dr-amal-almalki-an-inspirational-author-and-professor/. The *Executive Women* magazine online article.
King Abdullah University of Science and Technology (2016). https://www.kaust.edu.sa/en/about/administration/board-trustees. Accessed on November 10, 2016.
King Fahd University of Petroleum and Minerals (2016). International Advisory Board. http://www4.kfupm.edu.sa/iab/members.html. Accessed on November 10, 2016.
Lebanese American University (2016).
http://www.lau.edu.lb/about/governance-policies/board/bot/members.php. Accessed on November 10, 2016.
P.S. (2013). Douze Libanaises Parmi les "100 Femmes Arabes les Plus Puissantes" de 2013, Arabian Business.
http://www.lecommercedulevant.com/node/21730.

Qatar University (2016).
http://www.qu.edu.qa/theuniversity/leadership/board_members.php. Accessed on November 10, 2016.
Saint Joseph University (2014).
https://www.usj.edu.lb/decouvrir/conseilsdeta.htm?code=221. Accessed on November 10, 2016.
The American University in Cairo (2016).
http://www.aucegypt.edu/about/leadership/board-trustees. Accessed on November 10, 2016.
The Nigerian Higher Education Foundation (2016).
http://www.thenhef.org/about-us/board-of-directors/. Accessed on November 10, 2016.
University of Balamand (2016). http://www.balamand.edu.lb/AboutUOB/Mission/Pages/BoardofTrustees.aspx. Accessed on November 10, 2016.

Madonna Salameh-Ayanian is an Assistant Professor at the Faculty of Business and Commercial Sciences of the Holy Spirit University of Kaslik (USEK). Her research revolves around Human Resources Management, notably in areas related to the careers of women. In addition to being a lecturer on related topics, she heads the International Human Resources Management Master Program with Panthéon-Assas Paris II, and is the Head of the Corporate Relations Unit at the Faculty of Business and Commercial Sciences at USEK.

Diala Kozaily holds a Master of Sciences degree in Business Administration with an emphasis on Finance from the Holy Spirit University of Kaslik, Lebanon. She is also a Manager at Maison Kozaily SARL, a company that produces and distributes a variety of natural foods and beverages to the Lebanese market. She is currently finalizing her candidacy for a Ph.D. in Business Administration.

The Role of Religious Organizations Running Higher Education Institutions in the Arab World in Governance Reform

Georges Azzi

Introduction

In the twenty-first century, all countries are fighting to establish or preserve a position on the world map through higher education.

In the Arab world, the critical situation in terms of public policies and laws and their application make the challenge of achieving autonomy and transparency difficult. The higher education institutions in the region have barely modernized their governance structures in accordance with the ongoing changes.

On the one hand, higher education institutions in the public sector depend heavily on high-level state authorities, and thus the governance in those institutions is slow and rigid. Moreover, the effect of bureaucracies on curricula, degrees, and teaching regulations makes reform challenging. Additionally, at all institutional levels, actors are subject to the authority of the state. Some positions—university

G. Azzi (✉)
Holy Spirit University of Kaslik (USEK), Jounieh, Lebanon
e-mail: georgesazzi@usek.edu.lb

© The Author(s) 2018

171

G. Azzi (ed.), *Higher Education Governance in the Arab World*,
DOI 10.1007/978-3-319-52060-5_9

deans, for example—are directly nominated by government authorities. The head of a higher education institution not only is not sufficiently accountable to the university and society, since he/she has no impact on the process of selection or retention, but also is not in control of the financing and income, which are in the hands of the minister of finance.

On the other hand, it is true that private universities operate under a different hierarchical system, although in some countries their admission procedures are controlled by the government: The central government unit receives candidate applications and makes decisions about the affiliation of each candidate. Furthermore, it is obvious that these procedures have wide societal consequences.

The Arab world trusts private initiative in all fields thanks to several success stories. The education sector includes examples of a number of ownership structures, including single businessmen, family entrepreneurs, and religious organizations.

In the examination of the politics and social concerns of the Arab people, religion is a critical issue. Furthermore, religious organizations have considerable power in society, since they play the role of a political reference. They can influence, either directly or indirectly, the laws and regulations in a given country and/or in the whole region. Religious diversity in the Arab world is a double-edged sword: It can put pressure on an already critical situation, but at the same time it can be a source of social, intellectual, and cultural enrichment. Religious organizations are involved in the provision of many services to society, such as health (through opening and managing hospitals) and education (through successful schools and universities).

Given that governance reform is a must and religious organizations are important units of power in the Arab world, what would be the role of religious organizations in governance reform in higher education institutions in the Arab world? In order to answer this question, we begin by studying the current situation. We then go on to highlight the limitations and problems for governance and conclude by giving some recommendations based on a futurist perception.

An Overview of Religion and the Presence of Religious Organizations in the Arab World

Significant Existence

In the Arab world, religion is not limited to an individual's private relationship with the sacred as determined by a set of beliefs and doctrines expressed through specific rituals and practices. It is a matter of belonging, social status, and worth. In other words, in the Arab culture, religious belonging is an asset that is carried from birth and defended until death. Thus, given its importance and meaning, it is a taboo subject for social stereotyping.

Furthermore, declaring an attachment to a certain religion in the Arab world is not sufficient; religions are subject to subdivisions that might be, to a certain extent, more significant. In addition, in Arab culture and for a majority of people, denominations are reflected in their personality, attitude, behavior, and personal worth. Religious belonging might become a supplemental "nationality" for people, alongside that related to their mother country. For example, a Lebanese citizen does not only feel a sense of belonging to the Arab world and to Lebanon. He/she is also a Maronite, a Sunni, a Shia, and so forth. The same can be said for any Arab community. In addition, virtual borders can be created by religious and denominational diversity. Even sometimes within the national borders of an Arab country, religious subdivisions impose themselves and divide people by creating further diverse belongings and attachments.

Religious diversity can be considered a positive force in unifying the Arab world. A person from a certain religious denomination feels related to another Arab person from the same denomination in another Arab country. Thus, beyond one's Arab identity, a religious type of linkage can be highlighted, creating a sense of fraternity among the Arab world.

Then again, it can also be considered a direct or indirect source of divergence, conflict, disagreement, and misunderstanding, as well as a source of racism and discrimination in the same Arab countries and across the Arab world. Therefore, an inter-religious dialogue has been established to limit the negative impact of religious diversity by focusing on similarities without highlighting differences.

When discussing religious diversity, a critical issue comes to mind: the correlation between the percentages of people belonging to a certain religion or denomination and the impact, influence, and importance of that religion or denomination in the Arab world, at both local and international levels. In practice, each religious denomination, even if it is in the minority, has its own rules, regulations, tribunals, and judges. In other words, they differ in the degree to which they participate in the governance of the country. In some cases religious parties are running the country, while in others they have a specific role in parallel with the government. It is clear that the role of religious organizations cannot be marginalized.

Influence in People's Everyday Life

In the Arab world, religion is important not only from a theoretical perspective, but also in everyday life. In fact, religious parties are involved in many activities related to people's daily lives.

Religious parties contribute to people's well-being by providing health assistance through hospitals and/or dispensaries that they own and/or manage. These hospitals have a good reputation and prove themselves in the market on a daily basis through the assistance they provide. Many were established long ago and provide a professional service, spanning from the administrative to the medical staff. The question then arises whether health centers owned and managed by religious organizations offer their services for patients from diverse religious and denominational backgrounds?

Influence in Politics

It is clear that religious parties have an impact on Arab domestic and foreign politics. The relationships among different Arab countries might be determined by religious connections, which might lead to positive solid cooperation or negative divergent interests at the global level. It is important to acknowledge the relationship between modernization and governance. If governance consists of continuous development for the country, and if, in one way or another, religious organizations are in charge of any national governance, a simple conclusion can be reached concerning the need for continuous modernization at the religious organizational level. Indeed, an underdeveloped religious organization could lead the country backward and cause serious damage to fragile Arab countries.

The degree to which religion influences politics in Arab governments differs from one country to another. Some Arab countries are ruled by religious parties. In others, they influence the government, rules, and regulations in different ways. Ministers in some Arab countries are elected on the basis of religious affiliation; this affects their behaviors and actions, since they are representatives of the nation and, at the same time, are elected by a certain group. If this were not the case, could the nations preserve their diversity or would they be dominated by the same cultural religious group? Further to this, public positions are divided up according to religious shares or quotas. Do they preserve diversity, or do they decrease the effectiveness and efficiency of public entities, which should serve the country and its people? Would graduates and qualified students then choose to serve their country and express their attachment and belonging to their motherland? Is this the reason for the brain drain that the Arab world have experienced in the past?

Since religious organizations play a role in the governance of the Arab world, their influence can be seen clearly in the rules and regulations of many Arab countries. If the country is not ruled based on religious convictions and religious parties do not aspire to regulate the national governance, religious parties play their part in the judicial body. In many countries, personal status laws are managed by religious parties. People report to a justice tribunal according to their denomination. For example, in most Arab countries, civil marriage does not exist; people marry according to religious rules in reference to their denomination. In most regions of the world, a nation of human beings who live within the same territory, have the same origin, and share the same history, culture, and language, obey a common law. This is not true in the Arab world, since every denomination is subject to its own personal status laws and regulations. For instance, in the Lebanese territory, a Lebanese Muslim man has the right to register four marriages, but a Lebanese Christian man can legally only marry one person. The same logic applies to inheritance law, especially the inheritance of daughters. This can be seen in a positive light, if religious organizations are playing their role and taking responsibility in the absence of efficient government. In contrast, it can be seen as a way of imposing their presence and power. This issue can be subject to many other interpretations, depending on which factors are considered, that are of major interest for further study and research.

The existence of a correlation between democracy and certain religions has been the subject of multiple studies that have highlighted historical connections between religion and politics. Some religions influence both society's organizations and individual ethics. In an Arab context, the evidence of an intersection between culture and politics is very persuasive. There exist divergent views about the impact of religion on democracy. Some scholars contend that religion has a negative impact on democracy, arguing that some religious parties promote intellectual conformism and uncritical acceptance of beliefs and authority. Other theologians view religion as a supporter of democracy according to its own interpretation. Based on this point of view, religious parties participating in or shaping the politics of a country are more accountable and less subject to criticism. Therefore, in all religions, both fundamentals and elements that are not favorable to democracy can be found. Since any religious issue is subject to different and also divergent interpretations, even within the same religion, some dissimilarities might occur.

The impact of religious orientation on political attitudes and practices has been the topic of several studies by scholars in the USA. Some have concluded that there is a strong and positive correlation between personal religious convictions and conservative positions concerning public strategies related to ethics and moral issues. Other studies suggest that, in general, individuals seeking religious directions support military and defense-related expenses (Tessler 2002). Many studies relate gender to the degree of influence by religious beliefs. In some Arab countries, women's personal faithfulness clarifies the relationship between religious attachment and democracy. Not from a purely scientific point of view, but leaning more toward humanitarian enlightenment, some Arab people, dissatisfied with the existing political order, may shift to an alternative that combines democratic principles and optimal responsibilities with the religious conviction of justice and the protection of weak people (Tessler 2002).

Tessler (2002) suggests that in Morocco and Algeria, women have more negative feelings about the status quo than men and are dissatisfied with the present socioeconomic situation. Therefore, they prefer rules and regulations related to religious education about justice, equality, and social prosperity. Furthermore, a cross-regional comparison shows that the influence of religion on political orientation is more frequent and consistent in the West. In spite of all the studies and research concerning this subject, further analysis on different levels is needed to understand the degree of impact and the way religious convictions influence the democratic scene.

It is impossible to discuss the role of religious parties in politics without mentioning extremists and their influence. From the West to the East, it is recognized that extremism and radicalism have not just appeared today, but are the cumulative result of events experienced over a certain period of time. Those religious parties aspire to participate in the current governing life. In some countries in conflict, some extremist religions are working to establish a place in the new shape of the country, even though they are not necessarily recognized as active political entities; in some cases, their presence is not even recognized by the law, while in other cases they are legally only allowed to work in a socio-religious context. In the areas they control, extremists are applying their rules and regulations and even requiring and imposing by force general and specific education based on their beliefs and convictions.

The Current Situation in the Education Sector

Since 2003, the Arab world, which is committed to ensure the welfare of its population, has been investing in its education sector. The number of universities in the Middle East and North Africa region has more than doubled, reaching 398, without taking into consideration colleges, training centers, and non-affiliates institutions (Wilkens 2011).

Studies show that public universities are more dominant in the Arab world than private and non-governmental universities. However, a number of studies suggest that this general rule does not apply in every instance, since in some countries—such as Bahrain, Lebanon, Palestine, Qatar, and the United Arab Emirates—the proportion of non-public universities exceeds 80%. In Lebanon, there is only one public university—the Lebanese University—with different branches, some of which do not offer all majors. In Algeria, Iraq, Libya, and Morocco, on the other hand, private universities account for less than 20% of universities (Wilkens 2011). Many of the newly established universities are nonprofit institutions. The region has witnessed the development of many foreign branch campuses and the launch of free trade educational centers—the Knowledge Village in Dubai is a typical example.

Private universities have different ownership structures and management forces, such as families and religious organizations. It must be highlighted that universities owned and/or managed by religious organizations are numerous and exert power over the whole sector. In the Middle East, Islam, Christianity, and even minority religions affect the education sector through their education bodies, which teach their creed, and/or through the choice of majors.

The influence of religious organizations on the decision-making of higher education institutions that they own and operate is an interesting topic. In addition, they indirectly affect the decisions made in non-religious higher education institutions, and the rules and regulations in the whole sector, by being a strong competitor and through their explicit power. Most of the time, religious people do what they consider true and correct in their institutions.

Furthermore, higher education institutions follow the American model by having a vision and mission that forms the identity of the organization and distinguishes it from its competitors by defining its objectives.

Evidently, the universities that follow the French model do not have mission statements, since the concept does not exist in their system (Akonkwa and Lowe 2015) and some tasks are identified by the law and are common to all universities; in addition, each newly appointed president follows their own plan. According to studies that have examined the mission statements of several universities in different Arab countries, it is noticeable that some higher education institutions owned and managed by religious organizations, such as in Lebanon for example, have moderately rich mission statements. But even in those universities, when the mission is compared with ongoing activities, dissonance and exaggeration can be found.

It is true that a large number of mission statements are unadaptable, and in the case of some higher education institutions in the Arab world, their mission statements have been well formulated and published in various media channels and in different languages.

In fact, some missions and visions mirror the religious organizations more than the university itself. The higher education institutions might not be the main target, but might be a weapon for religious organizations to preserve their presence and influence in the Arab world. Under those circumstances, the absence of an effective strategy and a clear vision and mission statement are explicable.

In addition, in the Arab world, many universities have a poor international reputation; that is why considerable efforts are being made at the regional level to enhance the quality and even the image of the higher education bodies. Indeed, local initiatives are being implemented to create regional quality assurance and accreditation commissions. In Bahrain, the Quality Assurance Authority for Education and Training (QAAET), established in 2008 by a royal decree, is developing indicators for quality assessment and stressing the importance of transparency and accountability through published reports. In the United Arab Emirates, universities' adherence to international standards of quality is monitored by the Commission for Academic Accreditation (CAA). The oldest institution concerned with quality in the Arab world is the Accreditation Council in Jordan, which was established in 1990. It was replaced in 2007 by the Higher Education Accreditation Commission, which gained more financial and administrative independence. In Kuwait, special attention is given to private universities, since the Private Universities Council is responsible for managing the establishment of new private universities and developing criteria and conditions for academic accreditation. In other words, private universities in Kuwait are directly and closely monitored by the Private Universities Council. Consequently, Arab universities, especially those managed by religious organizations, are cooperating with these and many other bodies in order to establish good reputations. Furthermore, according to academic rankings of universities worldwide, in 2015, four universities in Saudi Arabia and one in Egypt were ranked among the top 500. Since in some Arab countries religious and governmental bodies overlap, it will be difficult to differentiate their influence in relation to the worldwide rankings.

Arab universities are not only seeking to gain local accreditation or to appear in the international rankings. Nowadays, international accreditation for universities or faculties is a must for higher education institutions. University accreditations are conducted by specialized organizations. These professional institutions assess the university against specific and predefined criteria for a certain period of time. It is a periodic assessment that aims to improve global academic performance and influence the whole education market. For example, the European Foundation for Management Development's Quality Improvement System (EQUIS),[1] the Association to Advance Collegiate Schools of Business (AACSB),[2] and the Association of MBAs (AMBA)[3] are well-known, professional, and reputable international accreditations for business schools. Many Arab universities are aiming to gain accreditation to enhance their presence on the world educational map.[4]

If the majority of universities are aware of the importance of international accreditations, why are there so few accredited Arab universities? It is true that Arab universities are aware of the need for quality and the importance of international accreditation, and accreditation is perceived as fashionable. Nonetheless, many challenges need to be overcome. Among those highlighted by university directors, professionals, staff, and other stakeholders in many studies conducted on the subject in the Arab world are significant budgetary needs, the divergence between the local culture and the international standards proposed, and the awareness of all stakeholders of the importance of obtaining this

---

[1] EFMD EQUIS accredited. More information can be found on its official website: https://www.efmd.org/accreditation-main/equis (accessed December 2016).

[2] AACSB international. More information can be found on its official website: http://www.aacsb.edu/accreditation (accessed September 2016).

[3] Association of AMBAs. More information can be found on its official website: https://www.mbaworld.com/accreditation (accessed December 2016).

[4] For a list of Arab universities and their relative accreditations, see: http://www.al-fanarmedia.org/2015/05/internationally-accredited-schools-and-institutions/ (accessed December 2016).

recognition. All these limitations are in one way or another related to governance in higher education institutions. We assess these and other governance problems in the next section.

A few Arab universities owned by religious organizations are internationally accredited. For example, in Lebanon, the Holy Spirit University of Kaslik (USEK) worked hard to acquire the German accreditation Evaluationsagentur Baden-Württemberg, known as Evalag. Since the governance of a higher education institution is influenced directly by the body owning it, and religious organizations wield significant power, especially in the Arab world, religious organizations can be expected to have greater influence on governance not only in their higher education institutions operating in the Arab world but also within the overall system.

Limitations and Problems for Governance

It is true that efforts have been made, changes have been implemented, and there have been many improvements in higher education institutions and their governance. But it is also clear that governance in higher education institutions faces problems and restrictions. This section is an effort to constructively evaluate governance in those institutions, in the most objective manner possible, in order to detect the system's weaknesses. It is very important to understand the reality if we are aiming to make improvements. Instead of searching for a party to blame, we should first consider it our role and duty, then that of all stakeholders jointly, to collaborate with the aim of improving governance in higher education institutions.

Limitations and Problems for Governance: Ownership and Management

One important subject is the ownership and management structure. A major governance problem is conflict of interest: The owner and the head of the board can in fact be the same person. Furthermore, studies of the higher education institutions in the Arab world conclude that there is an absence of clear standards for the selection process, evaluation of staff, and administrative and incentive systems. The law of "the right person in the right place" is not respected, since corruption and nepotism exist in educational institutions in the Arab world. Moreover, deans are appointed in the majority of universities. This process is subject to different types of influence, such as political considerations, that are related neither to education nor to competences; this deprives the faculty of independence and makes it somehow directly related to the owner's beliefs and visions, expressed through everyday activities. When discussing ownership and management, the board of directors (BoD) or trustees (BoT) must be mentioned. These governance bodies are not always present in higher education institutions in the Arab world. Efforts are being made to form them in some private higher education institutions managed by religious organizations; USEK, for example, formed its first BoT in the academic year 2015–2016, which met in 2016 in Lebanon on its main campus. Since the initiative is still in its early stages, it would not be helpful to evaluate its impact on governance reforms. Some institutions are nonprofit organizations sponsored by external parties. Do institutions managed by religious organizations benefit from religious financial support? In fact, religious entities may have shadowy objectives far beyond education facilities, whose achievements are attained to the detriment of the so-called goals. These higher education institutions are an effective platform for political activities and an instrument for ideological stimulation. In order to illustrate the idea, we refer to what happened in Turkey: the aborted "2016 *coup d'état*" and the imprisonment of academics and professors.

Limitations and Problems for Governance: Freedom and Decision-Making

Higher education institutions in the Arab world, whether or not they are managed by religious organizations, lack freedom. Public freedom and human rights ensure that individuals are at liberty to hold opinions and express ideas under the umbrella of academic freedom. Theoretically, universities are platforms that secure academic freedom for their students and entities in order to initiate open dialogue in which people express and defend their points of view on the basis of democracy, social norms, and public respect. However, it is well known that in this area of the world, many subjects are taboo, and in some countries there are serious consequences for discussing these subjects. Since this has been the case for a long time, it is difficult for some countries to implement democracy, even if it is possible due to some changes in the local and political power structure. For many reasons, such as the religious nature of the university and state control of private and public universities in some Arab countries, academic freedom is paralyzed; faculty members are oppressed and rarely participate in the decision-making process, and universities lose much of their potential for scholarly innovation, initiate no research creativity, and have less influence on the country's economic development.

In the Arab world, the deficiency of accountability and transparency is an epidemic that has spread to many sectors, including public and private higher education institutions. In this context, a question comes to mind: Do auditors exist? If so, what is their role? Are they efficient and working effectively toward professional higher education governance practice and reform?

Limitations and Problems for Governance: Students' Participation

It is not possible to discuss governance and not talk about students and their role as major stakeholders. Student clubs represent the voice of students. They are the link between the higher education institutions and student bodies, and they have the role of defending students and speaking on their behalf, claiming their rights and expressing their demands and requests. Their existence is a form of expression, democracy, and freedom. In the Arab world, in many higher education institutions, laws and regulations do not allow the creation of student clubs, which is an intriguing issue. Neglecting the role of students in decision-making processes is an obvious limitation of governance. Students lack the space to participate and influence the decisions of owners/managers of higher education institutions. The theory of social-oriented and student concerns might be unrelated to the everyday reality and practices, and might be reduced to philosophical issues. A dissonance therefore exists between rules and regulations, and practices and management.

Limitations and Problems for Governance: Financial Influence

Given the nature of higher education institutions as nonprofit organizations, the discussion of governance practices must highlight financial limitations. Since higher education institutions are, for the most part, not-for-profit organizations, institutions are financed through either public or private parties. In both cases, the budget is subject to external influence. Universities are not financially independent; they are influenced, in our case, by the religious organization that owns and manages the institution. This might be a double-edged issue. Being related to a strong body such as a religious organization might be beneficial to the institution, as the institution can absorb some of the organization's power, or it might be harmful, as the organization is detached from the institution's main objectives: education and research. Are budget allocations made for research purposes? Is research conducted freely and without constraints? Indeed, the university is subject to political, financial, and ideological forces.

Limitations and Problems for Governance: Quality versus Quantity and Philosophical Approach

Universities' practices and management in the Arab world are accused of being quantity-oriented, sacrificing the importance of quality in several areas. Due to the existing competition among universities (especially the private ones), financial constraints, and the pressure for international ranking, universities might privilege quantity and attempt to attract a large number of "customers." In the Arab world, a significant number of universities are prestigiously labeled as targeting the upper class. Paradoxically, monotheistic religions preach equality and target their institutions at the upper class.

Since the relationship between the higher education institution and the party managing it is reciprocal, the curricula might be affected by theoretical philosophical and theological studies. This might further distance the university from social reality and result in a separation between the university's concerns—their intellectual identity—and society's realistic preoccupations. Studies in the Arab world show a lack of conformity between the contents and purposes of programs and the skills needed by students to address social problems. If in general this threat exists, it appears the problem might be compounded in the case of universities managed and owned by religious parties, which might have an even greater tendency to be removed from the social environment. In order to stay up to date with those issues, universities should carry out continuous research, noting that the solution itself is a major concern for those types of universities.

Limitations and Problems for Governance: Research and Researchers

Research is a main component of governance practices in higher education institutions. Local and international higher education institutions are focused on developing their human, technological, and financial research resources. International ranking agencies and accreditation bodies encourage institutions to conduct more and better research projects. As religious universities are aligned with predetermined values and beliefs, the quality of their research might be of lesser value than that undertaken at other Arab or international universities or research centers. In particular, when the research is directly related to the belief system, it will not usually be able to meet international academic standards. The university should be a platform for improvement in technology and science, through committees and think tanks, engendering solutions for the problems affecting society. History has shown that religious organizations do not always stay up to date with scientific developments and findings. Therefore it is clear that research may be sacrificed in the interest of religion. One of the ways this is done is through constant threats of censorship or reduced budgets. In several Gulf countries, research concerning social, religious, cultural, and ethical issues are subject to significant restrictions (Morsi 1990). Taha-Thomure (2003) quotes an Algerian professor's reply to a question about academic freedom in Arab universities: "In Arab universities, instead of academic freedom, there are different levels and types of academic oppression." In medicine and biology, for example, scientific research might concern artificial insemination. The majority of the divine religion is against this practice. Are they willing to contribute to the development of science concerning a subject they don't even support? If they are, would the university or faculty be influenced by the beliefs, education, and religious background of the party to which they belong? Independent of their own point of view, their behavior is limited not only by the law, but also by their religious convictions, which might seem true and valid to some and obsolete to others.

Limitations and Problems for Governance: Religious and Social Beliefs

Instead of having a positive impact on improving human lives, religious universities might sometimes increase the negative effect of a social phenomenon, notably in the context of discrimination against women and the rate of enrollment of women in universities. In some Arab countries, religious organizations discourage female education. The proportion of literacy among Muslim girls (2/1,000) is much lower than that among Muslim boys (78/1,000) and Jewish girls (313/1,000) (Herrera 2007). Women in the Arab world have fought for the right to education and to join universities. In 2000, in some countries— including Egypt, Lebanon, and Iraq—women comprised half of the students of several faculties, such as medicine, which had previously been considered "male" specialties (Herrera 2007). In Saudi Arabia, Qatar, and Kuwait, and in the Arab Gulf countries in general, the proportion of women is approximately 50% of the undergraduate population, but they do not have full access to faculties and fields. In Saudi Arabia, under the Wahhabi Islam laws and practices, women are directed toward selected diplomas (teaching and social work) under the control of the Presidency General for Girls' Education. The number of women who have access to universities where the majority of the students are men under the Ministry of Higher Education is extremely small. We can conclude that religious parties affect the governance of education through the educational institutions they run in the Arab world, but also because they are part of the general politics and governance in certain Arab countries. In parallel to those Arab religious realities, it is possible to find other religious universities that are pioneers in female education and equality, such as the Syrian Protestant College, later named the American University of Beirut, and the University of Saint Joseph, both of which are foreign universities created by religious parties in the Lebanese territory.

Limitations and Problems for Governance: The Lack of Continuity between Colleges' and Universities' Curricula

A significant problem exists concerning the continuity between pre-university and university education in the Arab world. There is a lack of linkage between college and university programs. The university curriculum is not a continuation of the school program, and indeed it does not take into account the knowledge gained by students during their school years. Students experience difficulties in linking the scientific and epistemological modules to what they already know. This is in spite of the fact that, in the Arab world, some religious organizations run both schools/colleges and higher education institutions; hence, efforts are needed to link the curricula.

Recommendations

Education is currently an important topic in the Arab. The sector cannot be developed unless its governance is improved. Therefore, governance reforms in higher education institutions should be pursued as a priority. Despite all the difficulties that governance practices are facing, governance awareness and reform are finding their way into many sectors in the Arab world, especially in higher education institutions. The future is brighter, and more governance strategies, rules, regulations, and practices are being implemented. We expect that more universities will be practicing more and more governance. Some parties, such as religious parties, are expected to show more responsibility than others in this development, by virtue of the impact they have had and the potential they represent for the country. The Arab world has many resources and capabilities for achieving better opportunities.

Democratic standards should be established and fewer restrictions implemented. Entities running higher education institutions, in our case religious organizations, should promote certain principles, such as freedom, rights and fairness, freedom of expression, and knowledge creation through research. The education process and content should be independent from religious beliefs and practices but related to general ethics. Through their curricula and teaching techniques, religious parties should enhance university students' creativeness and openness and discourage routine learning and closed-mindedness.

The universities directed by religious organizations should function on an institutional basis and not a personal basis, promoting accountability and transparency. They should fight against the corruption that damages many sectors in the Arab world.

All religious entities should be able to critique themselves and tolerate others' criticism in order to develop in the sectors in which they are involved, including higher education institutions, through which they are supposed to be delivering knowledge. They should promote a culture of evaluation at all levels, including among administrators, faculty, and students.

Decision-making should be subject to mass participation; the role of both internal and external stakeholders should be robust. For example, elections are the obvious way to apply democracy. Professors and students should be able to found associations, clubs, and unions that work in their interest.

The governance of institutions should be put into good hands—not necessarily those of religious people, but those who are competent. Religious organizations accepting that they need to put civil non-religious people in key positions is a very important improvement. Professors, administrators, and others should be recruited and promoted based on their professional skills. A board of directors or a board of trustees should be created, which aims to implement better governance practices.

Religious organizations should influence the legislators in order to gain more freedom and independence as private higher education institutions. Moreover, they should switch from "top-down decision-making" to "open up university governance structures" (Wilkens 2011).

A university run by a religious organization as a nonprofit organization is encouraging for the autonomy of the university. Those universities need to search for more autonomy. When funding comes from different parties (governmental and private parties), no party can exert financial pressures or control. No restrictions would therefore be applied.

A quality system should be put in place and should involve different entities in the higher education institutions. It should include, for example, different training programs (professional, scholarly, and ethical) and should be applied to ensure good communication of all kinds of information. In addition, all types of needed resources should be provided in order that the institution can work effectively and efficiently. Moreover, curricula should be developed to cover scientific and technological developments. When higher education institutions managed by religious organizations in the Arab world apply a quality vision, they make their accreditation candidature and presence in international rankings possible. Governance practices can move the system from an educating to a learning system.

Religious organizations, which wield significant influence in the Arab world, should focus on improving higher education and scientific research in order to take advantage of the age of globalization. Religious parties concerned with the higher education sector can work in collaboration with all the parties in the field, such as the Association of Arab Universities; the Arab Federation for Technical Education; the Arab Federation of Councils for Scientific Research; the United Nations Educational, Scientific and

Cultural Organization's (UNESCO's) Regional Bureau for Education in the Arab States; the World Bank; the UN Development Programme (UNDP) Regional Bureau for Arab States; the Arab League Educational, Cultural and Scientific Organization (ALESCO); the Arab Bureau of Education for the Gulf States (ABEGS); the Arab Network for Open and Distance Education; the University of the Middle East Project (UME); and the Islamic Educational, Scientific and Cultural Organization (ISESCO) (Herrera 2007).

Arab cooperation has the potential to achieve different kinds of study, research, and publications. These, in turn, will enable different parties to share experiences and knowledge that can only have a positive impact on governance in the higher education sector.

Since higher education is a continuation of secondary school and religious organizations manage universities, more efforts should be made to improve governance. This continuity in the management party should be of great benefit for all parties, an added value that can generate continuity in the curricula and in university admission criteria and processes, as well as collaboration and reciprocity in improving the quality of education, and so forth.

All religious organizations are internationally linked to different parties. Those collaborations and connections should be for the benefit of the education entities they manage. In addition, collaboration among different religious entities and the universities they own is a must.

Principles and actions that steer in different or opposite directions reduce the intensity of the actions' consequences. Integrity is a necessity, especially when talking about humanitarian organizations, and indeed about religious organizations. Hence, it is important to provide scholarly charity that aims to deliver education to different social classes.

Religious organizations that run universities in the Arab world can take advantage of their education and business faculties, since they are the right parties to give advice on governance reforms in higher education institutions; business students, researchers, lecturers, professors, and deans are the preeminent internal stakeholders who can professionally and positively affect governance in their universities. The organizations therefore need to give them exceptional power and special status.

Organizations need to move away from theoretical philosophical education toward more practical education that can address current social concerns. Religious organizations need to fortify their presence and address various societal concerns, for example through research. The reform of governance in higher education institutions includes the bond between higher education and jobs. Entities that run higher education institutions, such as religious parties, need to exert extra effort in this direction.

Conclusion

The diversity of the Arab world is reflected in its higher education institutions. Both public and private universities, operating under different ownership and management structures, operate in the region. The governance philosophies and practices depend on the ownership structure. Different religious organizations operate and run higher education bodies, directly affecting the governance in their institutions and indirectly affecting the whole higher education sector. Major efforts are being made to reform higher education institutional governance. Since religious entities wield significant influence in the Arab world and are involved in higher education governance, religious organizations have a major role to play in higher education governance reforms. Many limitations and problems need to be overcome concerning such issues as ownership and management structures, students' role in the decision-making process, financial resources, quantity versus quality dilemmas, the gap between the philosophical and theoretical studies and the needs of society, research areas, discrimination against women, and the continuity between college and university studies. Religious organizations should promote democracy, fight corruption, evaluate work, integrate stakeholders in the decision-making process based on competence, make the governance structure more open, expand financial resources, put in place a quality system, keep up to date with scientific and technological developments, enhance Arab cooperation among different entities, create continuity between colleges and universities, use international connections, be humanitarian, give power to the education and business faculties, and move toward practical education. As Queen Rania of Jordan once said: "We need another revolution in the Arab world. We need an education revolution. If there's one thing we need to focus on, it's redesigning our educational systems."

Governance reform in higher education institutions is essential if university education is to enjoy a better future. It is impossible to talk about governance policies, planning, and practices in isolation from the current political, social, and economic situations in the Arab world, since the situation of the region is critical. Furthermore, the predominant presence and influence of religious organizations in the Arab world leads us to evaluate its influence on a larger scale. Hence, for any reform to be effective, it must be supported by political and social forces.

References

Akonkwa, D. B. M., and Lowe, R. L. (2015, August). A content analysis of European Universities' mission statements. In *Toulon-Verona Conference "Excellence in Services."*

Herrera, L. (2007). Higher education in the Arab world. In *International handbook of higher education* (pp. 409–421). Netherlands: Springer.

Morsi, M. M. (1990). *Education in the Arab Gulf states* (Vol. 28). University of Qatar, Educational Research Centre.

Taha-Thomure, H. (2003). *Academic freedom in Arab universities: Understanding, practices and discrepancies.* University Press of Amer.

Tessler, M. 2002 Islam and democracy in the Middle East: The impact of religious orientations on attitudes toward democracy in four Arab countries. *Comparative Politics, 34*(3), 337–354.

Wilkens, K. (2011). Higher Education Reform in the Arab World. The Brookings Project on US Relations with the Islamic World. 2011 US-Islamic World Forum Papers. Brookings Institution.

Georges Azzi is an Associate Professor of Finance at the Holy Spirit University of Kaslik (USEK). Former Dean of the Faculty of Business and Commercial

Sciences, he is currently Head of the Doctoral Commission at the Faculty of Business and Commercial Sciences, and the Vice President for Finance at USEK. He is also a member of the Editorial Committee of the Arab Economic and Business Journal (AEBJ), and has published several peer-reviewed articles.

Conclusion

Georges Azzi

Nowadays, we are living in a context of internationalization and globalization. Those concepts have a huge influence at the worldwide level; they affect the simplest details of daily life and the largest and most sophisticated economic and financial elements of the system. Therefore, higher education institutions in the Arab world, influenced by the phenomena of internationalization and globalization, aim to improve their quantitative and qualitative performance, and their international acquaintances and practices, to meet international standards. A large-scale change has begun, with the appearance of a global market without borders; significant mobility of people, especially of students; and the spread of cultures and their accessibility. These socioeconomic trends carry significant weight in relation to higher education governance. Higher education institutions in the Arab world have not attracted significant numbers of international students due to the region's insecurity and lack of political stability (IAU 2014). On the other hand,

G. Azzi (✉)
Holy Spirit University of Kaslik (USEK), Jounieh, Lebanon
e-mail: georgesazzi@usek.edu.lb

© The Author(s) 2018
G. Azzi (ed.), *Higher Education Governance in the Arab World*,
DOI 10.1007/978-3-319-52060-5_10

the number of Arab students aiming to study abroad has increased, to create an "inter-Arab mobility of students.". Given the factors noted here, the Arab world could have achieved better results in terms of internationalization.

Additionally, the challenges that higher education institutions in the Arab world are facing are not only those of internationalization and globalization, but also those associated with the fundamentals of governance. Some challenges come from within the institutions, such as adherence to traditional leadership, the dilemma of quality versus quantity, insufficient autonomy, and restricted sources of funding. Since an institution is not separate from its environment, its governance is subject to different challenges that are beyond the scope of its control, such as absence of reference in educational philosophy, lack of recognition for educational careers, political and economic instability in the Arab world, a mismatch between government and institutional educational bodies, misinterpretation of stakeholders' role, undervaluation of the role of education in societal change, and a shortage of reliable data in the field. These challenges, along with other actual boundaries, form the scope of work that higher education institutions should focus on through their governance experience.

Furthermore, higher education institutions are neither passive agents nor simple accepters of consequences. Institutions are considered to be more than communicators of information; they are a source of material creation, as initiators and generators of knowledge. Their governance impacts scientific research. Generally speaking, higher education institutions do not have freedom and autonomy from Arab governments—which worsens the strategic situation. The higher education sector is exposed to an increase in the number and diversity of students, changes in market demand, a questionable validity of resources, a rise in living costs, and budgeting cuts. As a consequence, the scientific research environment lacks a strategy and policies for achieving worthy and influential results. Furthermore, in the Arab world, the number of full-time university researchers is insufficient. Scientific discoveries are difficult to achieve in an atmosphere of poor informational exchange, databanks, and quality assessments (Meek et al. 2009). To deal with these realities, some Arab states of the Persian Gulf encourage the establishment of Western university campuses and allocate budgets for research purposes. In the absence of a comprehensive strategic plan, this effort is not a permanent solution.

Moreover, it is clear that higher education institution reform is a necessity. An institutional initiative would promote the reform of governance in higher education institutions. Since governance is a system of interaction, its absence or failure threatens academic transparency and accountability and fosters corruption (Mar'ie 2009). With fewer governance practices, faculties are less able to attract external financing, investment, and commercial partnerships. A lack of governance encourages an environment of unprofessional and unmoral practices and a lack of credibility. As a result, workers, administrators, and professors show less commitment in such an atmosphere, which lacks a clear vision of their personal development. It isolates universities from their societies' needs. In the Arab world, many universities do not have a clear educational philosophy. Management is based on obsolete, traditional methods, in which stakeholders' participation is marginalized. Instead of uniting forces, Arab universities search for assistance from foreign universities to solve their difficulties. Furthermore, Arab faculties are not keeping up to date with new educational trends and approaches, and some universities are still relying on the memorization of information in a heterogeneous curriculum, instead of innovative and analytical approaches. There is not only a lack of homogeneity in curricula, but also a schism between colleges' studies and universities' programs. Finally, universities, in the absence of practical, legal, and formal rules and strategies, search for the most effective and efficient alternatives when any critical situation arises.

Institutions are not the only important component in higher education governance. In fact, the institutional role in the governance process does not diminish the interaction between the government and higher education institutions in governance reform. The objectives of higher education institutions are not always in line with government interests; in the Arab world, the role of universities depends on the context of their establishment. Universities historically served religious organizations' interests. Then, colonial governments imposed their control on universities. Later, after the Second World War, the newly independent Arab regimes used universities as a source of power and human resource for their governments. As a result of major changes in the world in general and in the Arab world in particular, the "diversification" of the sector was initiated. The government, as a predominant controlling body, has different degrees of influence. It might intervene through its financial, legal, and social aspects, or it might play a more complex and direct role in universities' major decisions, such as the appointment of deans and student enrollment. It is not hidden from anyone that the intervention of the government in higher education institutions is not always beneficial for the sector. Excessive involvement, unclear policy, and insufficient budgeting inhibit the universities' ability to fulfill their duty. The link between the governance of higher educational institutions and the government is still rigid, noticeable primarily in terms of autonomy and the decision-making process adopted by universities.

A significant element of diversification in the higher education sector is the creation of private universities and the attraction of foreign campuses. Efforts to develop private universities in the Arab world vary among countries. In some areas, the large number of students graduating from colleges and belonging to middle-class families drives the sector to greater prosperity. This process is also beneficial to the government in terms of financial revenue. It reduces the pressure on Arab governments, especially with the oil crisis, since those universities are mainly financed via tuition fees. Private higher education institutions offer far more creative thinking and developed teaching and research techniques than public establishments (UNDP 2003). Likewise, instead of creating a change, Arabs have the predisposition to introduce foreign models and administrators from countries with outstanding educational systems. The goals and motives are two of the most important components determining the initiative's success. If the owner is aiming to achieve a prestigious higher education standard, institutions will be driven to work on international standards, creating a leverage effect on the governance practices of all competitors in higher education. On the other hand, if the objective of the owner is to quickly become profitable, the regulatory role of authorities will be more challenging and stakeholders' participation more restricted.

In addition, just as in other sectors in the Arab world, in higher education institutions women are facing salary divergences, limited opportunities, and social inequality (Inter-Parliamentary Union (IPU), 2014). A woman needs to understand the legislation that is currently applied to be able to fight for her rights. She needs to be an active agent to implement beneficial governance and change social stereotypes and perceptions by promoting herself as capable of confronting today's challenges. In order for women to do so, it is important to establish a suitable infrastructure, in which governance is the solution. Women are the first and most important party responsible for their current and future situation, and their sons and daughters should be raised according to principles of equality. By unifying, women can encourage and support each other to achieve more governance support.

Last but not least, some private higher education institutions are owned and managed by religious organizations, which directly affect the governance of their universities and indirectly affect the education system. Since religious entities exercise a great deal of influence in the Arab world, it is expected that they will play a prominent role in governance reform. University governance must address a number of challenges, such as management and ownership structures, decision-making processes, budgeting means, quality versus quantity concerns, philosophical approaches, research limitations, outdated social beliefs, and the discontinuity between colleges' and universities' curricula. In the process of reforming the governance of higher education institutions, the role of religious organizations will be to apply and enhance governance rules and practices.

As previously mentioned, it is important to discuss and analyze the challenges that our Arab-world universities are encountering every day in order to exert extra efforts that will lead to improved governance. Hence, our problem can be outlined as follows: What are the challenges that higher education institutions must overcome to achieve governance reform?

In such a critical situation, given the conditions in the Arab world and taking into account all that has been discussed throughout the chapters in this volume, it is obvious that it would be inconvenient and inappropriate to apply a Western model of reform in the Middle East and

North Africa (MENA) region. In order to be effective, the reform should be generated from within the region. We should create and shape a customized model of reform that suits the Arab region and its needs, taking into consideration its particularities: the convergence and divergence of different Arab countries.

Achieving the desired outcome will require not words but rather a sequence of continuous actions aimed at the same objective of improved governance in higher education institutions. Concerning globalization and internationalization, the Arab world are urged to apply two strategies: the reinforcement of the local training on offer, and the regionalization of their higher education institutions. Due to the particularities and constraints of the Arab world, these regions need to address the local market needs and students' expectations. In order to do so, universities must take into consideration the international dimension of their activities. Universities need to provide extra funds, promote economic influence, encourage tertiary education, and stimulate research and development (R&D). In order to encourage tertiary education, a larger number of students should be able to enroll in the related institutions, while relevant programs and curricula should meet the challenges of the labor market and a quality approach should be implemented. The internationalization of higher education institutions applies a scientific approach to the future and enhances informational and data resources, innovation and adoption of novel methods, and cooperation between different research projects. It is true that the Arab world has in common the Arab language. But there are many dissimilarities that make each Arab country a separate entity. Some countries have adopted the Anglo-Saxon system, while others are more French-oriented. Some countries are rich in oil resources, whereas others lack an oil supply. Given these discrepancies, the process and rhythm of internationalization differ from one country to another, and additional data will need to be collected in order to pursue comparative studies.

Moreover, if we continue to employ the current leadership and governance models, the challenges that higher education institutions are facing will be hard to overcome. It is neither easy nor impossible. It will be possible to promote governance reform if specific means are employed. A strategic plan powered by financial budgeting and effective leadership is a must. In addition, a common and shared vision is important to unify efforts to improve governance practices. An environment that promotes learning and the acceptance of change, in which professionals are constantly undergoing development, is favorable for governance reforms. Professionals, administrators, and staff members should be recruited from the best applicants. Students should not be bombarded with useless information. They should be engaged in holistic development: in civil, emotional, spiritual, ethical, academic, and intellectual improvement. Furthermore, programs and curricula should go beyond the simple transmission of information and include a diverse array of courses that include peace education, a learning approach, and the sharing of culture. Nowadays, with all the existing technologies, a traditional course or lecture is no longer conceivable; the correct use of technology is a must to endorse networking, partnerships, and so forth.

Governance practices are linked to high-quality learning through continuous formation and assessment processes. Moreover, governance creates a linkage between all stakeholders and involves different parties in the decision-making process. The education of students is not the mission of the educational body alone, but a complementary effort between educational bodies and parents. Institutions should encourage parents to pursue a problem-solving approach with their protégés. A governance model is never complete without a board of trustees, consisting of representatives of all stakeholders and the management body, who will create the governance rules and ensure their best implementation. To conclude, it is about a shared, "zero-based" governance model that can be transformed into an effective, transparent, and ethical structure.

Strengthening strategies need to be implemented in most higher education institutions, despite all the efforts that have already been made. Policymakers and specialists should promote an environment of academic and practical autonomy, and post-secondary education should be made available to a larger number of students. A research culture should be promoted through the mission statement, encouraged through policies and incentives, and stimulated through appropriate infrastructure and facilities. Research projects are not isolated from their environment, and hence ongoing research should be linked to socioeconomic development plans. Researchers should also be given special attention. In fact, the number of teaching hours for academics should be reduced in favor of more guided and well-managed research activities. Universities and research centers should work hard to attract "highly-skilled full-time [...] researchers." Human resources are of prominent importance in the research field, and financial resources are equally important. In fact, to retain qualified, passionate researchers in the Arab world, we need to maintain stable financial budgeting. Human and financial resources are not the only assets the Arab world needs in order to improve its research environment. Data and informational resources are also of great importance. Informational networking is a must for exchanges between researchers; a primary database is necessary for all fields; and quality assurance centers are guarantees of excellence.

We already mentioned the importance of institutional efforts in the reform of higher education governance. In fact, universities are laboratories in which future qualified leaders are prepared to take responsibility and search for solutions to social problems. To meet the current demand and overcome their weaknesses, higher education institutions must adopt a governance strategy. More precisely, the number of governors should be representative, and the governance members in the university and on the board of trustees, and the university size, should be balanced. With regard to the governance board, all committees and councils should be active in fulfilling their social and national responsibilities. Governance practices do not only involve the board; faculties also have a role to play, and they should therefore build professional partnerships with specialized parties. For example, the faculty of engineering should have partnerships with engineering companies, concerned governmental parties, and non-governmental organizations (NGOs) that are active in the field. Institutions compete for their administrative and financial independence through specific regulations that should be revised continuously. Governance is a culture to be shared with all stakeholders, such as students, faculty members, and administrative staff, to promote accountability and transparency. The reform of higher education institutional governance is a matter of "democratizing education" that promotes the autonomy of the university and its sustainable development.

Furthermore, focusing on the inconsistency between the implemented governance systems and the local culture can teach the Arab world a lot about the effort that should be deployed in order to foster a healthier future relationship between the government and higher education institutions. To achieve an "efficient governance system," a democratic environment is necessary in order to establish more autonomy for universities and give more influence to stakeholders in decision-making processes. By this logic governments should adopt a new, non-traditional role as moderated controllers and effective resource providers. This role will be characterized by distinctive, lucid, and long-term policies that are accompanied by clear practical methods, such as significant budget allocations. As important as the achievement of this shift in the government role is, the relationship between governance and democracy is the principal factor. Universities, as a platform for a utopian civil society, should promote a public interest approach among students according to which "open debate, and rational and critical thinking" are advanced. In the move toward this democratic "modern civil society," researchers are the guarantee of "pluralism and accountability" and the cultivators of free-thinking citizenship. Higher education institutions are the appropriate place to plan the future, with more positive awareness and less unconscious negativity, through the production of a rational "shared memory" purified of emotions. Consequently we can understand that bureaucracy and political regimes, either hidden or declared, remain the main "handicap for the implementation of a real higher education governance system."

In addition, higher education institutional reforms and privatization in the Arab world are of critical concern. The participation of faculty in the decision-making process has been shown to be important in both public and private institutions. Privatization might be a solution for governance in higher educational institutions. However, applying Western prototypes could damage the autonomy and authority in Arab academic institutions. Over time, the global higher education sector tends to stimulate a collaborative academic governance model. To ensure effective teaching results, instructors should enjoy autonomy in their classrooms. In addition, researchers should be able to freely choose their topics of study and take advantage of professional evaluation by outside experts. International regulatory agency executives promote and support these aspects of an independent environment. It is to be expected that an elaboration of these governance standards will be found in institutions seeking international accreditations and linking educational programs to social and economic reforms. All educational institutions are invited to follow this example in searching for quality enrichment. The privatization of higher education institutions in the Arab world, following international standards under local governmental authority, would be useful for achieving a truthful governance model in response to the pressure of creating a modern Arab university sector aligned with the rest of the world.

Concerning women and their role in higher education institutions, the "glass ceiling phenomenon" should be broken and replaced with real governance rules and practices. To do so, several actions need to be taken. Budgeting, as mentioned earlier, is a serious issue in educational governance; therefore, scholarships should be established to encourage women to develop their skills and thereafter gain positions in organizations. Laws are not set for a lifetime; they need to be revised and rectified to remain relevant. In particular, regarding the presence of women, quotas and practical strategies should be instituted to support and encourage the participation of women. Similarly, human resource (HR) policies and practices should be reformulated to take into account the work–life balance and gender equality policies. Women should maintain a continuous development process, especially in leadership and management skills. All the governance improvements already mentioned would not be sufficient if they were not complemented with a cultural shift at all levels, toward a modernized stable society.

To conclude, religious organizations, given the power they wield, are among the parties expected to take more responsibility and to influence positive governance in institutions. Religious organizations that own and run higher educational institutions should promote democracy and freedom of expression in order to boost creativity and openness. Their decision-making should not only reflect their point of view or interests, but also make room for the participation of stakeholders, such as students and professors. Those universities are invited to work on an institutional basis toward more accountability and transparency, tolerating constructive criticism and elaborating self-evaluation, such as a quality assessment system. To do so,

Index

© The Author(s) 2018
G. Azzi (ed.), *Higher Education Governance in the Arab World*,
DOI 10.1007/978-3-319-52060-5

CPI Antony Rowe

Chippenham, UK

2017-09-08 19:27